Wisdom Erases Karma. . . .

Brain/mind researchers have claimed the human mind has 200,000 times the capacity of the greatest computer ever built. That's an incredible untapped reservoir!

If your mind has even the capacity of a laptop personal computer, it shouldn't be difficult to accept that your Higher Self can direct you to a page that relates to your needs at this time. This book is a positive psychic symbol system—an oracle, not to tell your fortune, but to increase your free will. When you are aware of the unseen influences affecting your life, you can choose directions consciously to create your own reality. . . .

—Dick Sutphen,
from the Introduction

Psychic researcher, past-life therapist, and seminar trainer Dick Sutphen is the author of over four hundred self-help tapes and thirteen metaphysical books, including the bestselling *Past Lives, Future Loves; Finding Your Answers Within; Predestined Love; You Were Born Again to Be Together; Unseen Influences;* and *Earthly Purpose* (all available from Pocket Books). Dick Sutphen has appeared on many major television shows, and since 1977, almost 100,000 people have attended his world-famous seminars throughout the United States. Dick and his wife, Tara, live in Malibu, California.

Books by Dick Sutphen

The Oracle Within
Earthly Purpose
Finding Your Answers Within
Past Lives, Future Loves
Predestined Love
Unseen Influences
You Were Born Again to Be Together

THE
ORACLE
WITHIN

DICK SUTPHEN

POCKET BOOKS
New York   London   Toronto   Sydney   Tokyo   Singapore

An *Original* publication of Pocket Books

 POCKET BOOKS, a division of Simon & Schuster Inc.
1230 Avenue of the Americas, New York, NY 10020

Sutphen, Richard.
    The oracle within / Dick Sutphen.
        p.   cm.
    ISBN: 0-671-72360-X :
    1. Fortune-telling by books. I. Title.
    BF1891.B66S87   1991
    133.3—dc20   91-18625
                                   CIP

First Pocket Books trade paperback printing August 1991

10 9 8 7 6 5 4 3 2

POCKET and colophon are registered trademarks of
Simon & Schuster Inc.

Printed in the U.S.A.

To Tara, Scott, Todd,
Steven, Jessi, William, Travis,
Hunter, and Cheyenne—

a long lineage of love.

Many thanks to all the writers, philosophers and teachers who have influenced these writings—especially Will Schultz, Stewart Emery, Alan Watts, D. T. Suzuki, J. Krishnamurti, Bhagwan Shree Rajneesh (Osho), Sheldon B. Kopp, Lajos Egri, Robert Anthony, Joe Hyams, Jess Stearn, Ruth Montgomery, Brad Steiger, Bruce Lee, Don Weldon, Jimmy Moore, William Glasser, Ed Ford, Shoma Morita, David K. Reynolds, The Center for the Practice of Zen Buddhist Meditation and my own spirit guides and Masters who support my communication by sharing concepts.

Special thanks to the Bukkyo Dendo Kyokai of Minato-ku, Tokyo, Japan, for the kind permission to use their words.

Extra special thanks to my in-house editor, Sharon Boyd, to my agent, Susan Ginsburg, and to my Pocket Books editor, Claire Zion. We've all worked together on many books and they always find ways to make me look better.

Some of the words and concepts in this volume have appeared in books, magazines, and on audio and video tapes published by Valley of the Sun Publishing, Malibu, California.

Contents

THE
ORACLE
WITHIN

INTRODUCTION

Tarot cards, the I Ching, Rune stones and bones tossed by a tribal shaman are all psychic symbol systems whose purpose is to allow the awareness of your superconscious mind—the 90 percent of your mind you don't normally use—to enter your conscious mind. There is nothing magical about these systems. You could develop your own form of divination, perhaps by randomly dropping pine needles on the roof of a yellow Volkswagen when the moon is full. By developing a way of interpreting how the needles fall, you could draw knowledge from your superconscious.

Another name for the superconscious is the "Higher Self," the all-knowing level of mind that includes what Carl Jung calls the *collective unconscious*—human nature and cosmic order united in combined awareness. Eastern/New Age/metaphysical thinking believes we are all *one*. If we are all part of the collective unconscious, we are all connected, which explains why psychic symbol systems are so often accurate.

Most people claim to have had synchronistic experiences. For example, maybe you start thinking about a friend you haven't spoken with in months. You decide to call her. She answers the phone and says, "I don't believe this. I'm sitting at my desk writing you a letter." What happened? When your friend started thinking about you, your superconscious mind became immediately aware of it and there was some conscious "bleedthrough." You started thinking about her, probably because she was focused upon sending and you were in a receptive state of mind. Chances would be against it happening again the following day.

What if a stranger a thousand miles away started thinking about you? Would your Higher Self know it? Yes, but since there is no established "link" or closeness, you would not become aware of it consciously. If the stranger planned to come to see you, could a Tarot reading alert you to this? Of course. Your Higher Self is aware of everything that relates to you.

While conducting a Tarot reading I once told a friend, "You're going to sell your house and move away. It has to do with your work and you'll be making more money."

He had no plans to move at the time. But two weeks later he was offered a high-paying job in another state. He put his house up for sale and everything worked out as foretold in the reading. Why? Because the man who hired him had already decided to make the offer. My friend's Higher Self was aware of it, and through the psychic symbol system of the Tarot, it related this knowledge.

In another situation, I did a reading for a female friend. In the cards I saw that her husband was having an affair and the marriage would soon end. I didn't explain this to my friend because I didn't want to program her fears to become self-fulfilling prophecy in case the reading was wrong. But events unfolded exactly as I had foreseen. Her Higher Self knew what was happening and spelled it out.

Why isn't a psychic symbol system 100 percent accurate? Why is it sometimes dead wrong? Because most events are not predestined. A symbol system relates information based upon the potentials that exist at the time of the reading. My friend who received the job offer had the free will to refuse it. But free will is only a factor until you're *in the stem of the funnel.* Imagine a funnel, which has a wide mouth and narrows down to a long, narrow stem. While you're in the mouth you have free will—you're working with cause. But when you enter the stem you begin to experience effect until you come out the other end. In the stem there is no free will.

Consider this example: A married couple does not get along. As their fighting escalates, they are in the mouth of the funnel and have the free will to alter the worsening situation. But let's assume they just keep fighting until the wife decides she has had enough and she files for divorce. The husband doesn't want a divorce but he's in the stem of the funnel experiencing the effect he helped to create. Free will no longer exists in this relationship.

Or think about a man who smoked three packages of cigarettes a day for twenty years. He's been in the mouth of the funnel for a long time. He could have stopped smoking and his lungs would have healed. He had free will. But when he instead develops terminal cancer, he's in the stem of the funnel, experiencing the effects.

Brain/mind researchers have claimed the human mind has 200,000 times the capacity of the greatest computer ever built. That's an incredible capacity! Even if it only has a capacity equal to the greatest computer ever built, I'm impressed. It isn't hard to accept that mind can do some miraculous things.

Before you read any further I'd like you to stop and do something. Assume for a moment that you have the ability to read a half million words a minute. By slowly fanning this book back and forth a couple of times you will superconsciously read it. Please stop and do this now.

If you fanned the book while looking at the pages, your Higher Self is now aware of the contents. If you can believe your mind has even the capacity of a laptop PC computer, it shouldn't be difficult to accept that your Higher Self can direct you to a page that relates to your needs at this time. This book is a positive psychic symbol system—an oracle, not to tell your fortune, but to enhance your free will. When you are aware of the unseen influences affecting your life, you can consciously choose directions to create your own reality.

My favorite metaphysical principle is *wisdom erases karma*. In other words, if you are wise enough to change, you can probably mitigate or eliminate the need for some painful learning that awaits you in the future in the stem of the funnel. The following pages contain a lot of wisdom; I've had guidance from my Higher Self in writing this book. It contains the awareness of eighteen years of work in the metaphysical field as a psychic researcher, author, counselor and seminar leader. Even if you never consult these pages as an oracle, this book can still be used as a volume of metaphysical and human-potential philosophy.

HOW TO USE THIS BOOK
AS AN ORACLE

To consult this volume as an oracle you need a clear and concise question. If you don't have a specific question, simply ask, *"What do I most need to know at this time?"* Next close your eyes and breathe deeply. You can imagine, like I do, a beam of white light coming down from above and entering your crown chakra on the top of your head. This light is the universal light of life energy, the God light. Feel it filling your body to overflowing and then concentrating around your heart area. Next, visualize the light emitting from your heart area and surrounding your body in a protective aura. Silently say these words, *"I call out to the positive powers of the universe, and to my guides and Masters. Protect me in the white light of your love, from all things seen and unseen, all forces and all elements. Assist me to obtain awareness for my greater good. I thank thee in advance for your assistance. As above, so below. I ask it, I beseech it, I mark it, and so it is."* Now dwell upon your question for a moment before opening the book at random to read the message from your Higher Self. At the end of each reading are instructions for further clarifying the situation by referring you to other passages through simply tossing a coin three times.

After you've read the next passage you can again toss the coin for more clarification. However, do not ask for further clarification more than three times in regard to any one question or exploration in any one day. Also, do not ask the same question more than once a day! This is a rule in any divination system. If, after three referrals, your answer still lacks clarity, make sure your intent is clear. Exactly how did you phrase your question? What do you really want to know? Remember, too, your sincerity in asking will be reflected in the response.

Sometimes the book will answer your question from a broader perspective than you anticipated. If this happens,

5

accept that your Higher Self is aware of your spiritual goals and earthly purpose, even if you're not. Sometimes, when you compare your initial message with those you receive by tossing the coin, the two may seem paradoxical. Osho says, "Truth functions as paradox. To go beyond paradox is to go beyond intellect; the real understanding is always transcendental." So, if the messages appear to be paradoxical, attempt to view them as from a higher level.

We all judge based on our experiences. I believe the more you work with *The Oracle Within*, the more you will come to accept its wisdom. I wish you spiritual awareness and balance and harmony.

Dick Sutphen
1991

1
WHAT IS, IS

IT IS YOUR RESISTANCE TO WHAT IS THAT CAUSES YOUR SUFFERING. Freedom lies in the acceptance of what is, for when you recognize and accept unalterable realities as they are, you stop wasting mental or physical energy attempting to change what cannot be changed.

The Serenity Prayer says: "God grant me the serenity to accept the things I cannot change, the courage to change the things I can, and the wisdom to know the difference."

This doesn't mean to passively accept life. What you have the potential to change, go ahead and change. But recognize the things you can do nothing about and stop wasting your time complaining about them. Gravity exists, that's what is. Your mate is quiet and stubborn, that's what is. More often than not, we waste our time trying to change other people. It can't be done, unless they desire to change themselves. Trying to force them to repress who they really are won't work for long.

Meditate upon your resistance to what is, and the high price you pay as a result of your expectations.

For a related message that will further clarify the situation, toss a coin three times:

3 Heads = 222   3 Tails = 157
1 Head and 2 Tails = 232   2 Heads and 1 Tail = 181

2
VIEWPOINT

REALITY IS WHAT YOU EXPERIENCE, AND HOW YOU EXPERIENCE LIFE is based solely upon the way you view what happens to you. Your viewpoint is the deciding factor in whether you perceive life as a hostile experience or as a tranquil oneness.

What you might call a negative situation in your life is only a problem if you perceive it as a problem. You have the ability to transform the way you experience your life. As difficult as it might be to accept, your problems actually contribute to achieving satisfaction to your life. If there were no problems to challenge you, there would be no growth. You would have no way to learn how to handle things and become aware of your own capability for making your life work.

In fact, if you didn't have problems, you'd probably invent some to give yourself the opportunity to grow and learn. That is often what you do. You manifest problems subconsciously to create new challenges.

Many problem situations can be resolved with a change in viewpoint. Meditate on how altering your viewpoint could resolve your current problems.

For a related message that will further clarify the situation, toss a coin three times:

3 Heads = 6   3 Tails = 134
1 Head and 2 Tails = 173   2 Heads and 1 Tail = 153

3
KARMA

YOU NEED TO DECIDE IF YOU ACCEPT KARMA AS YOUR PHILOSOPHI-
cal basis of reality. It is one thing to say you accept karma, but
it is another to live your life as though you know it to be true.
Karma either is or it isn't. It cannot be a halfway proposition.

Everything you think, say and do creates or erases karma.
And this includes the motive, intent and desire behind every
thought and action. The unerring law of karma is always
adjusting and balancing as a result of your choices. Thus every
condition in your life is karmic: your body, your relationships,
your career, your level of success . . . everything.

Neither God nor the Lords of Karma creates your suffering.
You and you alone are responsible. *There is no one to blame for
anything.* If karma is self-created balance, then everyone who
has ever made your life difficult has done so because you
needed the experience as a karmic test or learning experience.
How could you blame others for what you set up?

When you respond to these trials with love, positive
thoughts or compassion, you pass the tests and rise above
your karma. If you respond with anger, blame or negativity,
you fail and will have to be tested again sometime in the
future.

For a related message that will further clarify the situation, toss a
coin three times:

3 Heads = 86   3 Tails = 75
1 Head and 2 Tails = 110   2 Heads and 1 Tail = 18

4
PAUSE

IT IS TIME TO PAUSE AND REFLECT ON ALL THAT HAS TRANSPIRED and the potential of what might come. Wait patiently while the universe shifts and the players maneuver. Many changes are taking place. Some you see and some are hidden from your view.

Your desires are caught up in the changes and there is little you can control at this time. Don't waste your energy attempting to push against the river, and do not respond to your fear-based emotions. Doing so will invoke the law of resistance, draw the undesirable into your life and perpetuate its influence upon your reality.

The situation may last a few weeks or months, but light will appear at the end of the tunnel if you are aware enough to recognize its presence. Success will eventually come to pass, although it might not manifest itself as you expect. In the meantime, be aware of self-actualized principles: Karma is the basis of reality, and it is your resistance to what is that causes your suffering. Conscious detachment frees you from karmic effects. Your viewpoint dictates how you will experience your life.

For a related message that will further clarify the situation, toss a coin three times:

3 Heads = 99	3 Tails = 30
1 Head and 2 Tails = 121	2 Heads and 1 Tail = 132

5
DENYING OTHERS

YOU NEED TO UNDERSTAND THAT WHAT YOU DENY TO OTHERS WILL be denied to you. What you deeply believe defines your experience. What you feel strongly about and what you say creates your reality. For example, if you resent wealthy people, you'll never be wealthy. If you are irritated by other people's success, you will be denied success. If you're jealous of someone else's loving relationship, you will be denied an ideal relationship.

Negative emotions work against you because you can't attain that which you resent. Your negative attitudes program a cause and effect response in your subconscious mind—karma. The purpose of karma is to teach and in this case, to instruct you by denying you what you would deny others. Karma is trying to show you your attitudes are based upon emotions you need to transcend.

Meditate upon how this relates to your question. Consider your deep beliefs and how your own attitudes may be indirectly denying you what you want. What changes do you need to make to get what you want?

For a related message that will further clarify the situation, toss a coin three times:

3 Heads = 60   3 Tails = 121
1 Head and 2 Tails = 226   2 Heads and 1 Tail = 89

6
AN ENLIGHTENED PERSPECTIVE

ZEN MASTER NANSEN SUGGESTED THAT ENLIGHTENMENT IS NOT anything beyond the world. He said, "Those who are enlightened 'liberate' themselves not from the world but from their own deluded minds, which force metaphysical distinctions upon the world. If it is a cow, it is a cow; if it is a moon shining through the window, it is moonlight."

Consider looking at your current situation with "everyday eyes." Although you seek to detach yourself from undesirable worldly concerns, your acceptance of self-actualized ideas does not free you from the inevitabilities of existence on the material plane. Peace of mind will come through acceptance of what is, and becoming at one with the circumstances. If events are beyond your control, that is what is. Don't waste your energy attempting to change what cannot be changed. Instead, become one with the experience. If you are sad, be completely sad. If you are angry, be completely angry. If you are frustrated, be completely frustrated. Then let it go and get on with your life.

Contemplate how viewing your question with everyday eyes will serve you, and how the acceptance of what is can help you to get what you want.

For a related message that will further clarify the situation, toss a coin three times:

3 Heads = 56   3 Tails = 67
1 Head and 2 Tails = 74   2 Heads and 1 Tail = 230

7
CHOICES

CONSIDER THIS STORY ABOUT CHOICES: A MAN KEPT A GOOSE IN A bottle, feeding it until it grew too large to get through the bottleneck. But how could he get the goose out of the bottle without killing it or destroying the bottle?

This Zen koan offers a choice between two alternatives, both of which are equally impossible. The purpose of the koan is to reflect the dilemma of life—the problem of passing beyond the two alternatives of assertion and denial, both of which obscure the truth. The real problem is not getting the goose out of the bottle, but rather getting ourselves out of it. The goose represents man, the bottle, his circumstances. Our bottleneck is our conditioned way of seeing things. We see situations and problems as alien objects standing in our way rather than as an extension of our own consciousness. We are conditioned to believe that our mind is inside us and that our perceptions of the world are outside. Actually, our mind is outside and all that we perceive is within our mind. To put it another way, "The goose is out!"

Consider your current choices as self-created extensions of your own consciousness.

For a related message that will further clarify the situation, toss a coin three times:

3 Heads = 215	3 Tails = 121
1 Head and 2 Tails = 69	2 Heads and 1 Tail = 127

8
PERMANENT LOVE

THERE ARE FOUR TRIED AND TESTED STEPS TO MAKE YOUR RELA-
tionship whole and lasting:

1. Do things together. Activity builds a strong foundation for a good relationship. These activities should be other than having sex or watching television together. Get out and exercise together, work on a shared hobby, socialize or do something similar.

2. Continue to do things you do naturally and well. Individual activity is essential for the personal development of each partner. Always challenge yourself with new learning that will support your self-esteem.

3. Conversation. Take time for honest verbal communication in which real sharing takes place.

4. Work out your difficulties. Compromise and mutual confrontation of problems is critical to a successful, long-lasting relationship.

Meditate on your relationship and what you can do to strengthen and renew your union.

For a related message that will further clarify the situation, toss a coin three times:

3 Heads = 53   3 Tails = 232
1 Head and 2 Tails = 73   2 Heads and 1 Tail = 177

9
CONTROL

WHEN YOU ATTEMPT TO CONTROL AND MANIPULATE OTHER PEO-
ple, you express fear and establish extremely destructive negative interaction.

There are eight primary ways people manipulate others. First
is *guilt*, which is always used to hurt or to control. *Anger* is
especially effective against those unnerved by openly aggressive behavior. *Criticism* and *insecurity* upset someone's balance
by attacking their thinking or behavior. *Obligation* is often in
the form of an unspoken agreement. In other words, "If I do
this for you, you'll have to do this for me." *Withholding* is a
primary manipulative ploy used in close relationships. *Helplessness* allows a manipulator to claim he can't do what he
needs to do, unless you do what he wants you to do. *Teasing*
appears loving and affectionate on the surface but is a way
for the teaser to make an indirect statement. *Questions* can be
manipulative when the person asking the question already
knows the answer.

Meditate upon how this relates to your question. Who do
you attempt to control or manipulate? Who manipulates you?
What needs do you have that are not being met? Exactly how
are you acting disharmoniously? What immediate actions can
you take to create more harmony?

For a related message that will further clarify the situation, toss a
coin three times:

3 Heads = 198   3 Tails = 155
1 Head and 2 Tails = 135   2 Heads and 1 Tail = 44

10
LIFE PATTERNS

ALTHOUGH YOU PROBABLY DON'T REALIZE IT, STRONG BEHAVIORAL patterns have been established in your past. A good place to begin exploration is in your primary relationship patterns that continue to emerge. For example, the moment your mate is critical of you, you close down and refuse to communicate. Or when you are finally assured of your mate's love and dedication to the relationship, you become bored. There are common patterns of manipulation, including resistance, affairs, neglect and more. Meditate upon your relationship and sexual patterns.

An example of a career pattern is allowing only a limited level of success before doing something to cancel it out. Another is allowing frustrations to build up until a change is enacted. Meditate upon your career patterns.

If you discover strong life patterns that work against you, realize that they will continue to surface and rule your life until you make a conscious decision to change. To alter your patterns of behavior, you must break the fearful chains of illusion that keep you bound to undesirable past programming. It begins with awareness and a self-actualized viewpoint.

For a related message that will further clarify the situation, toss a coin three times:

3 Heads = 122   3 Tails = 100
1 Head and 2 Tails = 203   2 Heads and 1 Tail = 113

11
HIDDEN JEWEL

A ZEN STORY FROM BUKKYO DENDO KYOKAI TELLS OF A MAN who fell into a drunken sleep. His friend stayed by him as long as he could but when he had to leave he hid a jewel in the man's clothing in case the drunk might be in want upon awakening. When the drunkard recovered, not knowing that his friend had hid a jewel in his garment, he wandered about in poverty and hunger. Months later the two men met again and the friend told the poor man about the jewel and advised him to look for it. It was still there in an obscure jacket pocket.

Like the drunken man of the story, you wander about suffering in this life, unconscious of what is hidden away in your inner nature—pure and untarnished enlightened awareness. You have the answers you require within yourself. You have the wisdom to rise above any and all distress. You have the awareness to view your life from a detached perspective of unconditional love.

Meditate upon how this story relates to your life, and upon how to put your awareness into practice.

For a related message that will further clarify the situation, toss a coin three times:

3 Heads = 94   3 Tails = 175
1 Head and 2 Tails = 243   2 Heads and 1 Tail = 55

12
FREEDOM

YOU SEEK FREEDOM OF THE SELF AND FROM THE SELF, FOR THIS IS the ultimate goal. Freedom *of* the self means literal freedom—freedom from oppressive environments and relationships, the freedom of a satisfying career and the freedom to make your life meaningful. Freedom *from* the self is a matter of rising above the effects of all fear-based emotions, such as anger, selfishness, hate, repression, greed, envy, guilt, insecurity, egoism, prejudice and blame.

Accept that you are neither your body nor your mind, but a fully self-actualized soul who is living on earth to resolve your karma. All unresolved karma amounts to unresolved fear. All fear is fear of loss in the future. Your primary fears are your key karmic lessons. You have the opportunity to work through these fears in your quest for total freedom.

The best way to resolve your fears is to master your life. Although you are afraid, act anyway. Choose to fully experience your fear, while observing every internal reaction of discomfort. By allowing the fear to be, it lets you be and you negate the law of resistance. You rise above the effect of the fear; it simply disappears.

For a related message that will further clarify the situation, toss a coin three times:

3 Heads = 245	3 Tails = 46
1 Head and 2 Tails = 174	2 Heads and 1 Tail = 223

18

13
ALIVENESS

WHEN LIFE ISN'T AS FULFILLING AS YOU WANT IT TO BE, IT IS TIME to explore your level of aliveness. Aliveness is excitement, enjoyment in doing what you do. It's that blood-pumping exhilaration, challenge, joy, stimulation, and pleasure that makes life worth living.

Have you traded security for freedom and aliveness? Is your life running on momentum? If so, life has probably become so routine and dull you have to look for places to hide. Some people become couch potatoes addicted to TV, others gossip on the telephone. Some go to bars or seek out other empty distractions.

You need to know your mind can't accept a mundane reality for long. Eventually, it will subconsciously create some excitement to make life more interesting. It might generate a fight with your lover, make you sick, cause you to have an accident, or create some other kind of complication. It can generate circumstances that will result in the destruction of your relationship, health or career just so you'll have the challenge of rebuilding it.

Consider adding some joyous new challenges to your life before your mind does it for you. However, simply keeping up with all your responsibilites to others and increasing an over-commitment to work are not to be considered joyous challenges.

For a related message that will further clarify the situation, toss a coin three times:

3 Heads = 194	3 Tails = 99
1 Head and 2 Tails = 247	2 Heads and 1 Tail = 198

14
WHAT OTHER PEOPLE THINK

SOCIETY IS SET UP TO PRESSURE PEOPLE TO FIT INTO A UNIFORM mold. As a result people wear the masks of proper attire, manners and etiquette. They become conventional characters responding to the expectations of others—so concerned with what other people think they lose their own identity.

Do you project who you really are, or are you the person others want you to be? Some people won't have anything to do with you unless you are what they want you to be. But if you consider that logically, it means that these relationships are based solely on your willingness to be manipulated. Unless you comply, you'll be rejected. And the expectations of others will mold, dominate, cripple and paralyze you. Do you need that kind of a relationship?

Explore your question as it relates to the way you respond to what other people think. Do you need to stop repressing who you really are? If you did, what is the worst that could happen? What is the best that might happen?

For a related message that will further clarify the situation, toss a coin three times:

3 Heads = 28   3 Tails = 87
1 Head and 2 Tails = 135   2 Heads and 1 Tail = 125

15
NONACTION

ALTHOUGH YOU ARE ANXIOUS FOR THINGS TO HAPPEN, THIS IS A time for nonaction. Remain open and receptive to those closest to you because they can show you what you may be unable to see for yourself. You are dealing with some powerful karmic realities that must be traversed carefully. Someone else is manipulating circumstances behind the scenes, and if you become aggressive, a struggle is sure to have undesirable consequences.

Nonaction means being patient, cautious, and keeping profile. This is a time to practice self-awareness and to test your potential for self-actualization. To judge others is always a mistake, for there is no way for you to fully understand all the forces that have set the actions into manifestation. Blaming others is also a mistake because karma has established the current situation as a test for everyone involved. How do you pass the test? By allowing the principle of unconditional love to guide your thoughts, words and deeds as you play your role in this scene.

Meditate upon obtaining a higher understanding of all that is involved and remaining harmonious under the present circumstances.

For a related message that will further clarify the situation, toss a coin three times:
3 Heads = 51   3 Tails = 173
1 Head and 2 Tails = 147   2 Heads and 1 Tail = 31

16
THE LAW OF RESISTANCE

WHAT YOU RESIST YOU DRAW TO YOURSELF. AS LONG AS YOU resist something, you are locked into combating it and merely perpetuate its influence in your life. Resistance is fear, something you need to karmically resolve. You must let go of the fear by encountering it until you learn to consciously detach from what you view to be negative.

You must learn to yield to an oncoming force in such a way as to render it harmless and, at the same time, change its direction by pushing it from behind instead of resisting it from the front. A Master of Life doesn't oppose things, nor does he attempt to change circumstances by asserting himself against them. Instead, he goes with the flow, yielding to its full force and either pushing it slightly out of direct line or moving it around in the opposite direction without ever encountering its direct opposition. This is the principle of controlling life by going along with it.

How does this wisdom relate to your question and how can you incorporate it into your situation?

For a related message that will further clarify the situation, toss a coin three times:

3 Heads = 85   3 Tails = 230
1 Head and 2 Tails = 33   2 Heads and 1 Tail = 56

17
ONE PROBLEM

ONLY ONE PROBLEM EXISTS BETWEEN HUMAN BEINGS: FEAR. FEAR is responsible for all disturbances, large or small, international or interpersonal. And there is only one fear—the fear of being unable to cope with a situation. Do you believe you fear rejection? It isn't really rejection you fear; rather you fear being unable to cope with it. Are you afraid of rattlesnakes? Similarly, it isn't the snake you fear, but coping with such an encounter.

Say you're out in the desert and you're afraid of meeting a rattlesnake. You encounter a snake, then you're afraid it's going to bite you. It bites you, then you're afraid you're going to die. Each new aspect of your fear relates to a future potential, not the situation of the moment. You never fear what is; you only fear the future possibility.

Fear paralyzes you and keeps you from acting when you need to act. It can stop you from making a growth choice when it would be in your best interest. In accepting your fear and accommodating it, you are imprisoned within it.

Meditate on how the fear of coping relates to your question and how it keeps you from making choices that would serve you in the long run.

For a related message that will further clarify the situation, toss a coin three times:

3 Heads = 250	3 Tails = 6
1 Head and 2 Tails = 234	2 Heads and 1 Tail = 81

18
RISKING

LIFE UNFOLDS AS A SERIES OF TASKS TO ACCOMPLISH WHILE RE-
solving your karma and fulfilling your dharma. Without
strength-producing activity in your life, you'll become
depressed. Without risk you cannot grow.

Helen Keller said, "Security is mostly a superstition. It does
not exist in nature, nor do the children of men as a whole
experience it. Avoiding danger is no safer in the long run than
outright exposure. Life is either a daring adventure or
nothing."

In regard to the risk you're considering, you must ask yourself these important questions. Can you define the purpose of
the risk? What is the best that could happen if you risk successfully? What is the full potential loss? Does it involve the fear
of loss of love, control or self-esteem? Would you be risking
to please someone else? Can you reach your goal in another
way? Do you need more information before acting? Could the
risk result in a more honest, freer life? Is it a growth step that
could improve the quality of your life?

For a related message that will further clarify the situation, toss a
coin three times:
3 Heads = 123   3 Tails = 15
1 Head and 2 Tails = 84   2 Heads and 1 Tail = 210

19
THREE KINDS OF PEOPLE

ACCORDING TO THE BUKKYO DENDO KYOKAI, "THERE ARE THREE kinds of people in the world. The first are those who are like letters carved in rock; they easily give way to anger and retain their angry thoughts for a long time. The second are those who are like letters written in sand; they give way to anger also, but their angry thoughts quickly pass away. The third is those who are like letters written in running water; they let abuse and uncomfortable gossip pass by unnoticed; their minds are always pure and undisturbed.

"There are still another three kinds of people. The first are those who are proud, act rashly and are never satisfied; their natures are easy to understand. Then there are those who are courteous and always act after consideration; their natures are hard to understand. Then there are those who have overcome desire completely; it is impossible to understand their natures."

Meditate upon how this relates to your question and upon the kind of person you are and the kind of person you want to be.

For a related message that will further clarify the situation, toss a coin three times:

3 Heads = 236   3 Tails = 29
1 Head and 2 Tails = 191   2 Heads and 1 Tail = 41

26

20
LOVE & FEAR

FEAR IS THE PROBLEM AND LOVE IS THE SOLUTION. LOVE IS THE power and fear is the weakness. Bearing this in mind, consider your primary relationships.

Many of us are jealous, possessive and envious, yet we claim this is proof of our love. But can a possessive or envious individual really love, or is he protecting his own pleasure and thus operating out of fear? All too often, romantic love is rooted in fear—the fear of losing. In addition, where there is fear, there is aggression. Many love relationships include a great deal of aggression. A love relationship based on need is based on avoiding loss. But this only engages the Law of Resistance—if you're resisting loss, you automatically begin to program what you hoped to prevent.

Ideal love is unconditional. It is love without judgment, expectations or blame. Your love would not be dependent upon being loved. You would not expect your mate to change, to be something he or she was not. You would find joy in the other's happiness. Only when there is love for oneself can there be love for others. To experience loving yourself, you need to know and accept who you really are beneath your fears.

For a related message that will further clarify the situation, toss a coin three times:

3 Heads = 194   3 Tails = 247
1 Head and 2 Tails = 74   2 Heads and 1 Tail = 19

21
IMPERMANENCE

MAN SUFFERS BECAUSE OF HIS CRAVING TO POSSESS AND KEEP FOR-
ever things which are essentially impermanent: his own person, loved ones and material objects. All these are impermanent,
and as soon as man tries to possess them, they slip away. This
is like trying to grasp water—the tighter you clutch, the faster
it slips through your fingers.

Those who possess are themselves possessed. They are
slaves to their own illusions about life. Possessiveness is a
denial of the right of people and things to live and change.
Thus, the possessor actually loses.

A Master of Life abandons the desire to possess because he
understands that no one can possess and nothing can truly be
possessed. He no longer grasps at things that flow by in the
stream of life. Instead, he goes with the flow of the current,
becoming one with it, aware that all things are simply waves
in the water and to try to gather them will only make them
disappear.

Meditate upon what you are attempting to possess and upon
accepting what is.

For a related message that will further clarify the situation, toss a
coin three times:

3 Heads = 80   3 Tails = 39
1 Head and 2 Tails = 134   2 Heads and 1 Tail = 179

22
CONSCIOUS DETACHMENT

A PROBLEM DOES NOT NEED TO BE ELIMINATED TO BE RESOLVED. Often a better solution is a change in viewpoint. When you are no longer affected by a problem, you no longer have a problem, although nothing may have outwardly changed.

If you get upset when someone verbally berates you, it is because you can't separate things in an enlightened way. It isn't what someone says or does to you, short of physical violence, that affects you—only your thoughts about what they say affect you. Why allow another's lack of balance to affect yours? Why allow another's problem to create a problem within you? By accepting what they say you only hurt yourself.

Let's say the person closest to you is often warm and loving, and you enjoy these times, but this person can also be selfish and self-centered. During those times, you consciously detach and let the negativity flow through you without affecting you. It is that person's right to be grouchy, and it is your right not to be affected. Nothing about the situation has changed except the way you view it.

For a related message that will further clarify the situation, toss a coin Three times:

3 heads = 74   3 Tails = 231
1 Head and 2 Tails = 148   2 Heads and 1 Tail = 3

29

23
NEW BEGINNINGS

NEW BEGINNINGS ARE ALWAYS A STEP INTO THE UNKNOWN. YOUR present environment may be one of chaos and total confusion, but it will evolve into a state of peace and growth. More than ever, this is a time to maintain your principles and draw upon your awareness of higher knowledge. Deal with your problems one at a time and act on the most important considerations first. There is no need to feel overpowered. You have the power and ability to resolve the disorder and establish a superior situation in the future.

New beginnings are an ideal time to move from an attached mind to a detached one. The vast majority of people on this planet live out their lives knowing only the attached mind, which fluctuates from positive to negative as outside conditions change—from happiness and joy down through neutrality, to the basement of emotions: depression, anger, hostility and fear.

A detached mind allows fluctuation only from positive to neutral as outside conditions change. You accept all the joy and happiness life has to offer, but your state of mind drops no further than neutral because you understand you can't control others or manipulate unalterable realities.

For a related message that will further clarify the situation, toss a coin three times:

3 Heads = 71	3 Tails = 212
1 Head and 2 Tails = 130	2 Heads and 1 Tail = 187

24
ON GETTING UPSET

ANY TIME YOU GET UPSET WITH SOMEONE, IT IS A SELF-CREATED karmic test to see how much you've learned and whether you'll need to be tested in the future. Did you respond to the situation with compassion or neutrality? Did you respond with anger or negativity? Until you learn that negative, fear-based responses don't work, similar future situations are assured.

Be aware that you got upset because you had expectations of approval or control—of attaining the approval of others or controlling their actions or reactions. Simply stated, your expectations conflict with what is. It would be impossible for you to be upset about anything if your expectations were not in conflict with the current situation.

Ask yourself, "Where do I get the right to expect others to be the way I want them to be?" You don't want them to expect you to live up to their expectations, do you? In the future, every time you start to get upset, remind yourself, "My expectations are in conflict with what is."

For a related message that will further clarify the situation, toss a coin three times:

3 Heads = 126   3 Tails = 16
1 Head and 2 Tails = 40   2 Heads and 1 Tail = 68

25
KARMIC SELF-PUNISHMENT

SELF-INFLICTED KARMIC PROBLEMS ARE SUBCONSCIOUSLY ADMINIS-tered as a teaching tool until you can forgive yourself. But you won't forgive yourself until you know on every level of your body and mind that you've learned your lesson and will never make the same mistake again. You can learn through love and wisdom, but you learn the fastest through directly experiencing the consequences of your actions. Thus, you do most of your learning through pain.

You painfully learn that stress, improper diet and lack of exercise cause illness. But if the undesirable condition isn't too advanced, having the wisdom to change your life-style can reverse the situation. You painfully learn that manipulating other people to get what you want results in relationship problems. But through learning what doesn't work, you learn how to master relationships. Past-life fears predestine limited success in your career. But through metaphysical explorations you might find the cause of your programming and release the fears so you can pursue success.

Your difficulties are the karmic lessons you need to learn. Some were predestined, and some are the result of how you've lived your life. Meditate upon the wisdom of erasing karma.

For a related message that will further clarify the situation, toss a coin three times:

3 Heads = 229   3 Tails = 22
1 Head and 2 Tails = 103   2 Heads and 1 Tail = 146

26
COMPASSION

COMPASSION IS A FEELING OF DEEP SYMPATHY OR SORROW FOR another's suffering, accompanied by a desire to alleviate the pain or remove its cause.

Ideally, when you experience compassion for another human being, you can help by creating conditions that will allow that person to alleviate his or her own pain. Although you may experience the anguish of another's suffering, you must live with the knowledge that you can do nothing to save someone from their pain. From a karmic perspective, we are all self-responsible, thus even pain is a choice and only the individual can choose not to experience it.

You may want to ask yourself three important questions. 1. Is this person willing to accept responsibility for this condition? 2. Is he or she willing to do something to resolve it? 3. Does the person know what to do? If the answer to the first two is no, there is little you can do. But if the answer to the first two questions is yes, then you may be able to help that individual create the space to rise above the difficulty.

For a related message that will further clarify the situation, toss a coin three times:

3 Heads = 70   3 Tails = 131
1 Head and 2 Tails = 208   2 Heads and 1 Tail = 62

27
JUDGMENT & TRUTH

YOU JUDGE EVERYTHING FROM YOUR VIEWPOINT. YOU CALL SOME-
thing right, wrong, moral, immoral, ethical or unethical.
Maybe several people, or even the majority of us, agree to call
it the same thing. But that doesn't make it truth. Rather, it is
only our perception of truth. Our agreement that something is
moral cannot change what it actually is.

There is no such thing as truth. "Truth" exists only as it
relates to you. According to Antoine de St. Exupery, "Truth is
not what we discover, but what we create."

Life is filled with philosophical truths that we commonly
accept and rarely challenge. Yet in many cases, these outdated
truths, notions, views, and moralities are restricting our lives.
If you do accept others' truths as valid, you accept restric-
tions—you accept traps. A trap is an assumption accepted
without challenge, one that will keep you enslaved until you
do challenge it.

Meditate upon any truths you are accepting that are holding
you back or making your life more difficult than it needs to
be.

For a related message that will further clarify the situation, toss a
coin three times:

3 Heads = 250   3 Tails = 22
1 Head and 2 Tails = 117   2 Heads and 1 Tail = 164

34

28
YOUTHFULNESS

SOMETIMES YOU ARE CONCERNED ABOUT YOUR AGE AND HOW IT relates to your circumstances and plans. You need to be aware that joy and harmony are youthful energies, while negativity and disharmony are aged ones. Always seek to be joyful and you will remain youthful. Your body will age in keeping with natural law, but your mind and spirit can remain forever young.

When you are youthful you are adventurous and you experience aliveness and excitement in whatever you do. Only someone youthful will take the risks that make life worth living. If you allow yourself to become old in spirit, you begin to fear losing and start to trade growth opportunities and challenges for security and comfort. The dread of loss makes you a prisoner of fear, and thus you lose your freedom.

Consider your actual age only from the time you start living youthfully, consciously, awake and aware. Seek the joy that will allow you to remain youthful to the very end of your life. This joy is not generated by people and things outside yourself—that feeling comes and goes as outside conditions change and is of no lasting value. True joy is found deep within yourself; it comes from being who you really are and doing what you are here on earth to do.

For a related message that will further clarify the situation, toss a coin three times:

3 Heads = 239   3 Tails = 92
1 Head and 2 Tails = 107   2 Heads and 1 Tail = 152

29
AWARENESS

AWARENESS IS MEASURED BY HOW MUCH YOU LET YOURSELF KNOW of your own truth. Many of your truths remain buried in the memory banks of your subconscious mind. The subconscious contains knowledge, understanding, talents and abilities. It also contains memories of those past events that make you feel guilty or fearful. Since you do not consciously know about them, you lack the awareness to rise above them. But, at the same time, you experience the effects of this undesirable hidden programming.

You must explore what motivates and restricts your progress in regard to your desires. Answers are never difficult when you begin to ask the right questions. You can no longer hide from the questions you need to ask yourself. Meditate on your subconscious programming. Before you go to sleep, ask for dreams that will assist you in understanding what is holding you back. Ask that the dreams be received literally, not symbolically. Ask that you remember them immediately upon awakening. Keep a pen and paper at your bedside to record your awareness.

For a related message that will further clarify the situation, toss a coin three times:

3 Heads = 115   3 Tails = 11
1 Head and 2 Tails = 239   2 Heads and 1 Tail = 94

30
PROBLEM/OPPORTUNITY

As you were thinking about your question did you view it as a problem? Some people see their problems as *problems*— they complain and worry and verbalize them over and over. The more they talk about their problems the more they program the negative reality into their subconscious minds. In the long run this just further complicates the situation.

Consider viewing your problems as opportunities—opportunities to learn and grow. The only difference between problem-oriented people and opportunity-oriented people is *attitude*. If you view your problems only as opportunities, you will no longer have any problems.

Motivational tests have shown 15 percent of success is attributable to talent, IQ or ability, and 85 percent of success is attributable to attitude. Attitude is the difference between the high achievers in life and all the others.

Meditate upon this information as it relates to your question and explore your own viewpoint of problems and opportunities.

For a related message that will further clarify the situation, toss a coin three times:

3 Heads = 135   3 Tails = 224
1 Head and 2 Tails = 173   2 Heads and 1 Tail = 55

31
HAVE FAITH

THERE ARE TIMES IN LIFE WHEN YOU MUST HAVE ENOUGH FAITH TO let go and stop attempting to manipulate your circumstances. Don't push the river. Don't resist what is. Surrender. Have faith there are reasons for what you are experiencing and they are beyond your understanding. Know that your destiny is not the only consideration—others are involved. Believe that in time you will learn why things are happening as they are.

Your concern is based upon fear, although you may not realize it. Fear manifests itself in many emotions such as anger, selfishness, hate, repression, envy, greed, anxiety, guilt, insecurity, vanity, resentment, and prejudice. From a Higher Self viewpoint, you are here on earth to learn how to let go of fear and to express unconditional love. So your present concern is an opportunity for spiritual growth—if you direct your emotions positively. If fear is the problem, love is the answer. Meditate upon how you can express unconditional love in this situation.

Trust is part of faith. Trust yourself. Trust your Higher Self. Trust God, and trust the outcome will be for the greater good.

For a related message that will further clarify the situation, toss a coin three times:

3 Heads = 10   3 Tails = 203
1 Head and 2 Tails = 217   2 Heads and 1 Tail = 64

32
NURTURING

YOU NEED TO TAKE THE TIME TO NOURISH YOURSELF AND OTHERS who are important to you. After food, clothing and shelter, emotional and psychological needs arise.

Everyone needs to love and be loved. We all need music, entertainment and hobbies. But spiritual needs are as important as any others. An undernourished plant will not flower, and spirituality provides nourishment from the source —overflowing energy with which to blossom and fulfill your purpose.

Meditate upon everyone in your life who needs you. Nurture your relationships with an appreciation for all that is supportive and fulfilling. Nurture yourself by exploring your needs and asking for your guides and Masters to assist you in manifesting that which serves the greater good. Explore your patterns of thinking. Do you view the glass as half empty or half full? Do you see the good and valuable in situations, or do you dwell upon the negativity? Can you reflect God in your viewpoint by expressing unconditional love?

For a related message that will further clarify the situation, toss a coin three times:

3 Heads = 211   3 Tails = 243
1 Head and 2 Tails = 64   2 Heads and 1 Tail = 142

33
NO INDECISIVENESS

IT IS TIME TO MAKE SOME DECISIONS ABOUT COMMITMENT. WHEN your intent becomes clear—to make a decision to obligate yourself to a person, a task or a concept—everything begins to fall into place if your direction is in harmony with the universe and your purpose. Once you have pledged this direction, things happen almost magically, as if you were a magnet attracting that which is needed. The key to this ultimate power is to *have no indecisiveness at all.* The greater your emotional desire, the more power you give to those on the other side who can assist you and the sooner you will experience the manifestation.

Your first commitment must be to know yourself and be your True Self. Then you can stop living with one foot in the safety zone, withholding full commitment. If you partially commit, you can experience only partial joy. Total commitment offers the potential for total joy. Maybe you're here on earth to learn that life is what you make it and is to be enjoyed.

Process yourself about your commitments by asking the right questions. Answers are never difficult if you're willing to stop hiding from the questions.

For a related message that will further clarify the situation, toss a coin three time:

3 Heads = 164   3 Tails = 192

1 Head and 2 Tails = 16   2 Heads and 1 Tail = 241

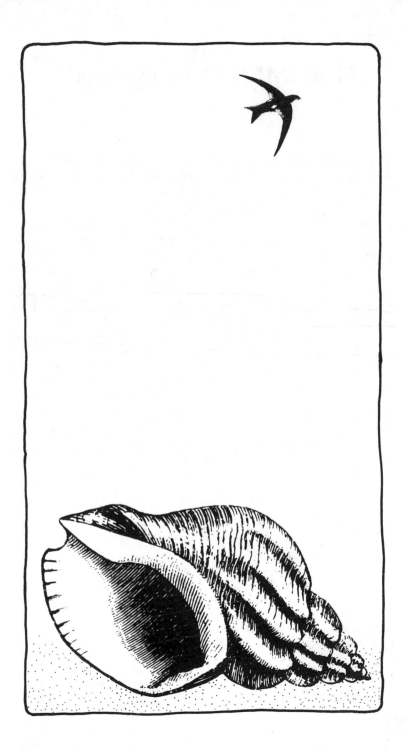

34
FRAGMENTATION & JOY

YOU, LIKE EVERYONE ELSE ON THE PLANET, ARE A MASS OF CON-tradictions. One part of you wants to do this, another part of you wants to do that. Pushed and pulled by internal desires, your personality is fragmented—and the result is stress.

But there is a way to deal with your fragmented being. As you spiritually evolve, you move deeper and deeper into your center until you reach your Higher Self and the collective unconscious. This is the God level. Joy emanates from deep within your center; when you experience joy you are never fragmented. To integrate yourself, all you have to do is do only what you enjoy. What would happen if you stopped doing the things you don't enjoy? For one thing, you'd remain centered at all times. You'd enjoy everything about your life.

Don't be irresponsible—learn to delegate. Work harder at what you do enjoy to earn the money to pay someone else to do what you don't enjoy. Maybe you'll have to sacrifice some security for more joy. If you're resisting the idea of living only for joy, you're probably limiting all your options in life. Meditate on doing only what you enjoy, and the changes you'd make if you decided to do it.

For a related message that will further clarify the situation, toss a coin three times:

3 Heads = 62	3 Tails = 118
1 Head and 2 Tails = 171	2 Heads and 1 Tail = 93

35
SELF-WORTH

You need to explore your feelings of self-worth. Universal Law says you can only attract that which you feel worthy of receiving. High self-esteem is critical to your happiness and success because you are a living expression of your belief system.

Your beliefs generate the thoughts and emotions that create all your experiences. Much of your present karma is the result of beliefs programmed by past-life events. But since karma is self-inflicted, it can be resolved only by self-forgiveness. Of course, this will come only as a result of your thoughts about yourself. Therefore, if you want to change your life, you must change your beliefs.

For example: If you want to be more successful in your career, you must accept the fact that your beliefs are restricting you. You need to understand that you *can't become what you resent*. If you resent people who are successful, you'll never allow yourself to attain success. If you feel hostile toward wealthy people, believing they are greedy or dishonest or selfish, you will never allow yourself to attain wealth. Why? *Because you will always live up to your self-image*. Meditate on your general beliefs and beliefs about self-worth as they relate to your question.

For a related message that will further clarify the situation, toss a coin three times:

3 Heads = 116   3 Tails = 91
1 Head and 2 Tails = 246   2 Heads and 1 Tail = 12

36
FIVE EVILS

ACCORDING TO THE BUKKYO DENDO KYOKAI, THERE ARE FIVE evils in the world. First is cruelty; every creature strives against another. The strong attack the weak; the weak deceive the strong; everywhere there is fighting and cruelty. Second is the lack of a clear demarcation between the rights of individuals. Everyone desires to be the highest and to profit at the expense of the other. They cheat and undermine one another. Third is the lack of clear boundaries in the behavior between men and women. Everyone at times has impure and lascivious thoughts that lead them into questionable acts and disputes. Fourth is the tendency for people to exaggerate their own importance at the expense of others, to set bad examples of behavior and, by being unjust in their speech, to deceive, slander and abuse others. Fifth is the tendency for people to neglect their duties toward others. They think too much of their own comfort and desires; they forget the favors they have received and cause annoyance to others that often passes into greater injustice.

Meditate upon how any one or all of these five evils might relate to your question and to your life.

For a related message that will further clarify the situation, toss a coin three times:

3 Heads = 25   3 Tails = 13
1 Head and 2 Tails = 133   2 Heads and 1 Tail = 170

37
LIVE NOW

YOU EXIST NOW AND NOW IS ALL THAT IS. NOW IS OUTSIDE OF time. There is no past in which you were incomplete, and there will never be a future in which you will become complete. Until you accept that you can only exist in the present now, you will believe that fulfillment awaits you in an illusory future if you take the proper actions. This belief destroys the experience of now and you continually live in illusion.

This very moment is it. Nothing is hidden. All your calculating and hoping and planning about how it will someday be, all your dreams and plans, this is how it all turned out. This is all there is. You've been planning all your life for the future, but you will never be aware of the future in the future. You will only be aware of it now. You do not exist in time. You exist in self.

Use the time component, but never allow it to entrap you in actions designed to achieve fulfillment in an illusory future. Be in the moment, fulfilled, perfect, at peace, and in balance. You have the power and ability to do this.

For a related message that will further clarify the situation, toss a coin three times:

3 Heads = 161
1 Head and 2 Tails = 154

3 Tails = 59
2 Heads and 1 Tail = 206

38
NOTHING TO SEEK

THERE IS NOTHING TO SEEK AND NOTHING TO FIND. YOU ARE already enlightened, and all the wisdom in the world will not give you what you already have. The truly wise seeker is concerned with becoming aware of what already is, the True Self that lies buried beneath lifetimes of fear programming.

The answers you seek will be found within as you explore who you really are. You probably think you already know yourself, but if you did you would know peace, balance and harmony. You would accept that what is, is—accepting unalterable realities without resistance. You would experience a detached mind—enjoying all of life's joys while allowing the negativity to harmlessly flow through you. You would accept karma as your philosophical basis of reality and would know that everything is exactly as it is supposed to be—though you can improve it. You would understand that reality exists as that which you experience, and the way you experience life is based on the way you view what happens to you. Your viewpoint is the deciding factor in whether you experience life harmoniously or disharmoniously.

For a related message that will further clarify the situation, toss a coin three times:

3 Heads = 175   3 Tails = 95
1 Head and 2 Tails = 208   2 Heads and 1 Tail = 123

39
YOUR ACTIONS

YOU ARE ENTERING A BALANCING CYCLE THAT OFFERS GREAT opportunities while also presenting some dangers. The outcome will depend upon your actions. Your feelings and emotions generate your thoughts, which are manifested in your actions. Therefore, chaos will be unable to affect you if your actions are the result of positive, harmonious feelings.

Your choice of friends and associates will play a major role in what is to come. It will serve you to examine the motive and desires of those closest to you, but do not get involved in their dreams and goals. Do not make any major emotional changes. Be extremely careful in matters of business. If problems occur with others, resolve the conflicts with unconditional love.

Through self-deception, you are often your own worst enemy. But you can also be your own best friend. Now is the time to step out of the darkness into the light of self-understanding. Explore what you have achieved thus far and work out a plan of action that will help you support your goals.

For a related message that will further clarify the situation, toss a coin three times:

3 Heads = 8   3 Tails = 139
1 Head and 2 Tails = 248   2 Heads and 1 Tail = 28

40
INNER STRENGTH

THERE IS NO WAY TO COMPROMISE NOW. YOU MUST STAND YOUR ground in a self-actualized manner by responding directly and honestly while detaching yourself from the negative aspects of the situation. Be assertive, stand up for your rights, but don't be aggressive by forcefully violating the rights of another.

Draw upon your inner strength and review your own motives. Every intended act generates karma, so be sure you are in harmony with the motive and desire behind your thoughts, words and deeds. As in every conflict, you have the potential for spiritual growth or to incur karmic debts.

Resolve the situation by following the watercourse way. A rock is strong in one way, water, in another. Water flows over, around and through obstacles without resisting them; it will eventually wear away the rock and turn it to sand. While the rock appears to be stronger, in the end it will be gone and the water will continue to flow.

For a related message that will further clarify the situation, toss a coin three times:

3 Heads = 160	3 Tails = 246
1 Head and 2 Tails = 151	2 Heads and 1 Tail = 53

41
BEING DIRECT & HONEST

YOU ARE OFTEN BOTHERED BY THE INTRUSIONS OF OTHERS. YOU resent the invasion of your privacy and the resulting waste of time. The more you resist these intrusions, the more you have to experience them, for what you resist you draw to you. If you'll examine the fear controlling you, you'll find it's based on an inability to cope with the situation.

To resolve the problem, all you have to do is to be honest and direct about what you want and don't want. Express your needs calmly, without resentment or hostility. Don't be afraid of hurting someone else's feelings. If someone cannot accept you as you are, without attempting to manipulate you, do you really need that person in your life?

When you are not direct and honest, you repress. But this repression will soon erupt in another form: you will take out your frustrations on someone else, or get a skin rash, headache or some other physical disorder. Repression is simply another expression of fear. Fear is negative subconscious programming that only creates future negative experiences. Life is more harmonious when you are direct and honest. In fact, the greatest gift you can give to another person is to be *all* of who you really are.

For a related message that will further clarify the situation, toss a coin three times:

3 Heads = 73   3 Tails = 176
1 Head and 2 Tails = 200   2 Heads and 1 Tail = 20

42
WISDOM ERASES KARMA

YOUR QUESTION OFFERS A UNIQUE OPPORTUNITY FOR GROWTH AND the potential to avoid negative karma if you act with wisdom.

You have the means to learn your lessons through love and positive action and mitigate your suffering. But sadly, we all seem to learn fastest through pain—through directly experiencing the consequences of our actions. After experiencing the pain again and again, lifetime after lifetime, we eventually learn what works and what doesn't.

For example, if we attempt to manipulate those closest to us we create relationship problems. After enough ruined relationships, we will finally—in this life or a future life—intuitively come to understand that we need to accept other people as they are without attempting to mold them into what we want them to be.

Consider these choices in all areas of your life: selfishness/sharing, greed/altruism, dishonesty/honesty, judgment/nonjudgment, attached mind/detached mind, blame/self-responsibility, expectations/acceptance. Meditate upon how wise actions relate to your question and how you can act to erase karma.

For a related message that will further clarify the situation, toss a coin three times:

3 Heads = 206	3 Tails = 54
1 Head and 2 Tails = 79	2 Heads and 1 Tail = 6

43
BLAME

YOU NEED TO LOOK AT WHO YOU ARE BLAMING, OR WHO YOU might blame if things don't work out the way you want. Blame is an expression of self-pity and is also incompatible with karma. Your past thoughts, words and deeds have created your present reality—good and bad. In other words, happiness and success are self-bestowed and unhappiness and failure are self-inflicted.

Karma is a system of absolute justice that creates the experiences you need in order for you to learn your lessons. Since you karmically create all your experiences, you can't blame anyone else. If your lover leaves you, it's a karmic balance from this life or past lives. If a business partner rips you off, it's balancing your deeds from another time and place. If someone in your life is driving you crazy, it's just a test. If you respond to your tests harmoniously, you've learned your lessons and probably won't have to experience similar tests in the future. But if you respond disharmoniously, you'll only create similar tests in the future.

You and you alone are responsible for everything you experience. Meditate on this self-responsibility as it relates to your question.

For a related message that will further clarify the situation, toss a coin three times:

3 Heads = 185   3 Tails = 151
1 Head and 2 Tails = 25   2 Heads and 1 Tail = 204

44
WORLDLY PASSIONS

THE BUKKYO DENDO KYOKAI SAYS, "THERE IS NO ONE WAY TO get free from the trap of worldly passions. Suppose you caught a snake, a crocodile, a bird, a dog, a fox and a monkey, six creatures of very different nature, and you tie them together with a strong rope and let them go. Each of these six creatures will try to go back to its own lair by its own method: The snake will seek a covering of grass, the crocodile will seek water, the bird will want to fly in the air, the dog will seek a village, the fox will seek the solitary ledges, and the monkey will seek the trees of a forest. In the attempt of each to go its own way there will be a struggle. But being tied together by a rope, the strongest at any one time will drag the rest.

"Like the creatures in this parable, man is tempted in different ways by the desires of his six senses, eyes, ears, nose, tongue, touch and brain, and is controlled by the predominant desire. If the six creatures are all tied to a post, they will try to get free until they are tired out and, then, will lie down by the post. Just like this, if people will train and control the mind there will be no further trouble from the other five senses."

Meditate on how this story relates to what you are seeking.

For a related message that will further clarify the situation, toss a coin three times:

3 Heads = 145	3 Tails = 73
1 Head and 2 Tails = 81	2 Heads and 1 Tail = 35

52

45
THE GREATEST GIFT

THE GREATEST GIFT YOU CAN GIVE TO ANOTHER HUMAN BEING IS to be all of who you are. Although you may not realize it, you're wearing masks to hide who you really are. Whenever you don't say what you want to say, or smile when you don't want to smile, or pretend to be someone you aren't, you're wearing a mask. The reason you wear it is fear. It's important to find out what you're afraid of, and to examine the price you pay. Often the masks aren't necessary. You're just wearing them out of habit.

There are hundreds of common masks: The workaholic mask usually helps you avoid something—maybe unwanted social contact or intimate interaction at home. The "poor little me" mask gives you something to talk about and gets you attention. The funny, gregarious mask helps you avoid things—real contact or intimacy—and it covers your insecurity. Exceedingly nice people feel uncomfortable if others aren't comfortable, or they wear this mask to pump their own egos.

When you are honest and direct there is no mask, no repression. Meditate on the reason why you wear masks, and know that a mask created to deflect pain and loss also deflects joy.

For a related message that will further clarify the situation, toss a coin three times:

3 Heads = 40   3 Tails = 159
1 Head and 2 Tails = 53   2 Heads and 1 Tail = 246

46
INSECURITY

LIFE IS INSECURE, LOVE IS INSECURE. THROUGHOUT YOUR LIFE YOU are always moving from the known to the unknown. You can resist insecurity but to no avail. Insecurity is based on the belief that you won't ever have enough: enough love, enough sex, enough time, enough control, enough success, enough attention or enough assurance that your relationship will last forever. You feel something is missing or impermanent, and you don't always even know what it is or why you feel what you feel.

But what if you could attain total security? Think about it. Anyone with any sense of adventure, drive or imagination at all would soon become bored. Your life would become dull and mundane. There would be no challenge—no aliveness. If you attained total security, the lack of challenge and aliveness would probably cause you to grow tired of the relationship. Thus your fearful emotions are not even logical because you wouldn't like what you wanted if you got it.

Meditate on your desire for security and explore the fears behind it. Ask to obtain an understanding of the cause of your fears during this meditation or in your dreams.

For a related message that will further clarify the situation, toss a coin three times:

3 Heads = 16

1 Head and 2 Tails = 95

3 Tails = 187

2 Heads and 1 Tail = 227

47
JEALOUSY

WHEN YOU ARE JEALOUS OF YOUR LOVER, YOU ARE EXCESSIVELY concerned that they are not as committed to the relationship as you want them to be. When you are jealous, you feel incomplete and believe that only through the relationship can you be complete. But stop, step back and look at this more carefully. You have to realize this viewpoint isn't logical. The relationship cannot make you complete. Excessively jealous people often feel they won't be able to survive without the other person, but that isn't any more logical than needing a lover to be complete. You know you'll survive, but your jealousy could actually drive your lover away because jealousy is always masked hostility.

Even if your lover truly is untrustworthy, you need to accept that you can't change your lover unless this person is willing to change. Sometimes the only way to be responsible to yourself is to remove yourself from the environment. But if you choose to remain together, you might as well accept your lover as is.

Meditate upon your feelings in the light of this awareness and upon your ability to accept others as they are, without expectations of change.

For a related message that will further clarify the situation, toss a coin three times:

3 Heads = 134   3 Tails = 205
1 Head and 2 Tails = 101   2 Heads and 1 Tail = 63

55

48
ACCEPTANCE

SINCE YOU CAN'T CHANGE SOMEONE ELSE WHO IS DRIVING YOU crazy, you might as well accept this person as he or she is. This other person isn't going to change, and that's what is. In accepting what is, you can find some peace. After all, it isn't logical to upset yourself when there is no value in doing so. The emotional drain will only result in negative subconscious programming, which will eventually make matters worse.

You have two choices: 1. You can get upset about someone and this person doesn't change; 2. You can choose not to get upset about someone and this individual doesn't change. The result is the same either way, but the choice is whether or not you waste your energy. You can detach and let it go. To continue to resist what you cannot change because you want to be right is ultimately self-destructive.

Consider the logic in this, and if you still have trouble detaching, meditate on your excessive need to be right.

For a related message that will further clarify the situation, toss a coin three times:

3 Heads = 119	3 Tails = 136
1 Head and 2 Tails = 42	2 Heads and 1 Tail = 24

49
DISHARMONY PROCESS

THE ONLY CAUSE OF KARMIC DISHARMONY IS FEAR. FEAR INCLUDES all the emotions that generate extreme negative responses, or paralyze you and keep you from acting when you need to. The action required to rise above this fear can include any or all of the following: 1. Acknowledge the existence of the fear; 2. Learn the reason behind the fear; 3. Seek out the cause of the fear; 4. Find the karmic action required to release the fear (i.e. self-forgiveness or retribution), and 5. Confront and fully experience the fear.

Explore primary fear areas: Who are you blaming? Who are you attempting to control? Who or what is causing you to become tense and anxious? Who or what are you resisting? Who do you hate or really dislike? Do you desire revenge? Who or what is causing you to become angry? Who are you jealous of? Whose approval do you need? What are your primary greed areas? What is your primary inhibition? What generates stress within you? Who or what frustrates you? Who do you envy? Who or what do you feel possessive about? Who or what causes you to feel insecure? Do you have any phobic fears?

Meditate upon how fear relates to your question and your willingness to answer these questions and act to resolve them.

For a related message that will further clarify the situation, toss a coin three times:

3 Heads = 174   3 Tails = 244
1 Head and 2 Tails = 83   2 Heads and 1 Tail = 104

57

50
OVERWHELM

YOU ARE CURRENTLY WITHIN THE EYE OF THE HURRICANE. YOUR environment has become the focal point of chaos because you continue to allow more and more into your life, resulting in the need for more time, more energy and more space to maintain order. The turmoil may be in your personal relationships or simply the cumulative effect of your interests and involvements. But you have to accept that you need to give things up in order to get what you want.

Since your days are full you must sacrifice in one area to make room for another. There is always a cost for what you want, and since you are overwhelmed by your current circumstances, you desire order and peace of mind. Begin with an accurate assessment of your current situation. Clarity of intent is the key to success. If you don't know exactly what you want, how can you expect to get it? Once the goal is firmly in mind, begin eliminating what no longer serves you. Don't rely on others to do this—it's your job. Pay close attention to details and begin to create the reality you desire to experience.

Meditate upon how this concept relates to your question. Visualize and plan for the return of a tranquil, harmonious reality.

For a related message that will further clarify the situation, toss a coin three times:

3 Heads = 176   3 Tails = 106
1 Head and 2 Tails = 65   2 Heads and 1 Tail = 77

51
CHANGING BEHAVIOR

LIKE EVERYONE ELSE ON THIS PLANET, YOU MUST FEEL WORTH-while—to yourself and to others—in order to fulfill your needs. This requires that you maintain a satisfactory standard of behavior, and correct yourself when you are wrong. If your conduct is below your own standards, you must correct yourself or you will subconsciously self-create a punishment—mental symptoms that could result in destructive behavior or physical ailments.

Explore your behavior to decide if it is working for you. If it is disharmonious, it needs to be changed. Changes in behavior also quickly lead to a shift in attitude, which can lead to fulfillment of your needs. You don't have to change how you feel about something if you are willing to change what you are doing. Change begins with action. Karma means action, and wisdom erases karma.

Nothing about yourself can be changed until it is first recognized and accepted. Because all disharmonious behavior is rooted in fear, begin your self-examination with four important questions: 1. What is the real fear? 2. What needs do I have that are not being met? 3. What am I doing that creates disharmony? 4. How can I change my behavior to create more harmony?

For a related message that will further clarify the situation, toss a coin three times:
3 Heads = 170   3 Tails = 169
1 Head and 2 Tails = 202   2 Heads and 1 Tail = 126

52
SEARCHING FOR HAPPINESS

YOU SEARCH SO HARD FOR HAPPINESS, BUT HOW CAN YOU FIND IT by searching for it? Happiness comes from within, the natural result of what you do in life. The more you spread joy to others, the more it will come back to you. If what you've been doing has not generated the joy and happiness you desire, it is time to change your approach. Stop searching. Stop desiring. Just *give*. Practice kindness. Share yourself. Give without expectations and it will be returned a hundred times over. Everything in life comes back to you.

Beneath your fears and insecurities, your true nature is pure joy. It isn't something outside that you can achieve, it is something inside you've forgotten—your essence—what you are and what you were meant to be.

When you compare your level of happiness to what you perceive to be someone else's level of happiness, you become dissatisfied, but the comparison arises from your ego and is always futile. You can't know how others relate to their lives. Everyone is unique. The person who appears to have it all may not be able to enjoy anything as much as you enjoy looking at a spring flower. When you stop comparing, you will experience *your* joyful essence.

For a related message that will further clarify the situation, toss a coin three times:

3 Heads = 156   3 Tails = 34
1 Head and 2 Tails = 168   2 Heads and 1 Tail = 193

53
FREE WILL

ALTHOUGH MANY OF THE EVENTS IN YOUR LIFE ARE ASTROLOGI-
cally predestined, you always have free will to mitigate the
impact of the event or to transcend it entirely. The path you
take is determined by two things:

1. How you've lived your life up until the destined experience: If you act with integrity and compassion, give grace and
mercy to others, are positive, loving and compassionate, you
may evoke the law of grace which supersedes the law of
karma.

2. How self-actualized you are: The more aware you are,
the less you will be affected by external events, because your
awareness allows you to let the negativity flow through you
without affecting you.

No matter what the experience, you always have the free
will to choose your response. The way you respond demonstrates whether or not you've learned from your past experiences and determines the need for similar lessons in the future.

Consider how this relates to your question and how you can
improve your response to the difficulties in your life.

For a related message that will further clarify the situation, toss a
coin three times:

3 Heads = 47   3 Tails = 62
1 Head and 2 Tails = 115   2 Heads and 1 Tail = 255

54
EXTERNAL THINGS

THE BUKKYO DENDO KYOKAI TELLS A STORY OF A TIME WHEN Shakyamuni Buddha was staying in the town of Kausambi: In this town there was one who resented Him and who bribed wicked men to circulate false stories about Him. Under these circumstances, it was difficult for His disciples to get sufficient food from their begging and they suffered much abuse in that town.

Ananda said to Shakyamuni, "We had better not stay in a town like this; there are other and better towns to go to; we had better leave this town."

The Blessed One replied: "Suppose the next town is like this, what shall we do then?"

"Then we move to another."

The Blessed One said, "No, Ananda, there will be no end in that way. We had better remain here and bear the abuse patiently until it ceases, and then we move to another place. There are profit and loss, slander and honor, praise and abuse, suffering and pleasure in this world; the Enlightened One is not controlled by these external things; they will cease as quickly as they come."

Meditate on how this story relates to your question and the way you avoid situations rather than deal with them.

For a related message that will further clarify the situation, toss a coin three times:

3 Heads = 61   3 Tails = 14
1 Head and 2 Tails = 70   2 Heads and 1 Tail = 101

55
THE LAW OF ATTRACTION

WHERE YOUR ATTENTION GOES, YOUR ENERGY FLOWS. YOU attract what you are and that which you concentrate upon. If you are negative, you draw in and experience negativity. If you are loving, you draw in and experience love. You can attract only those qualities you possess. If you want peace and harmony in your life, you must become peaceful and harmonious.

Are you clear about exactly what you want in each of the following areas: 1. Your primary relationship; 2. Your sex life; 3. Your relationship with family; 4. Your relationship with friends; 5. Your career; 6. Your level of success; 7. Your financial status; 8. Your expressions of creativity; 9. Your recreation and leisure; 10. Your spirituality.

If you are unhappy with what exists in any area of your life, you have the ability to apply the Law of Attraction to manifest the changes you desire. You will need to apply more positive energy to that area. You will have to be more committed to results. You may even need to change yourself so you can mirror the quality you desire to experience.

Meditate upon how the Law of Attraction applies to your question and your willingness to change to get what you want.

For a related message that will further clarify the situation, toss a coin three times:
3 Heads = 107   3 Tails = 166
1 Head and 2 Tails = 216   2 Heads and 1 Tail = 18

56
THE MIRROR

OTHER PEOPLE ARE A MIRROR FOR YOU TO SEE YOURSELF. THE TRAITS you respond to in others are ones you recognize in yourself, positive and negative. The mirror has four primary manifestations: 1. That which you admire in others you recognize within yourself; 2. That which you resist and react to strongly in others is sure to be found within yourself; 3. That which you resist and react to in others is something you are afraid exists within you; and 4. That which you resist in yourself, you will dislike in others.

In other words, you have chosen to reincarnate upon the earth plane to learn to rise above the effects of fear. Those fears, however, will always be reflected in your reactions to others. Thus your goals are very obvious once you are able to perceive them clearly. As you let go of the fear, it follows that you open to expressing more unconditional love.

Explore the manifestations of the mirror that are affecting your life at this time. What lessons can be learned by seeing yourself in these people?

For a related message that will further clarify the situation, toss a coin three times:

3 Heads = 177   3 Tails = 96
1 Head and 2 Tails = 38   2 Heads and 1 Tail = 14

57
DIVINE ORDER

IF YOU SEEK TO UNDERSTAND DIVINE ORDER, STUDY THE NATURAL balance of nature, for it works the same way. Everything is as it should be, although mankind is far from experiencing its potential for complete harmony. There are no accidents. Your energy, translated into thoughts, words, emotions, and deeds, causes all you experience. This assures that you always have the learning opportunities you need in order to resolve your karma. Also, the collective thoughts, words, emotions, and deeds of mankind create the environment for us all.

If enough souls focus their energy upon peace, we will have peace. If the majority of souls are filled with anger, we all may have to experience war. We are all one, and like the many subpersonalities within each of us, the dominant traits of mankind will emerge to resolve our group karma.

Meditate upon how Divine Order relates to your question and how you can use this understanding to act correctly and obtain what you desire. Consider, too, your collective thoughts, words, emotions, and deeds. How do they add up? Peaceful and loving? Neutral? Angry and negative? What does that tell you?

For a related message that will further clarify the situation, toss a coin three times:

3 Heads = 34   3 Tails = 138
1 Head and 2 Tails = 89   2 Heads and 1 Tail = 28

58
GATHERING

THE COSMOS IS DRAWING TOGETHER MANY OF US WHO SHARE THE same interests, bonds or goals—people with whom you have a past-life lineage. By combining your energy you will be able to serve yourselves and the greater good. You may be particularly drawn to specific people within this group. Allow this to happen, for it is destined to be. As the gathering becomes obvious, work to maintain unity and guard against the disharmony that could create karmic debt and weaken the commitment to accomplish these shared goals.

Those who are important to you in this life have been important to you before. You have reincarnated together to learn from one another and find new ways to express your creative potential. You were guided and maneuvered by unseen help, by your own subconscious, intuition, and by extrasensory abilities to seek out one another again. Once together the unlearned lessons from the past will surface, to be worked out and ultimately balance the karma and fulfill the dharma of all involved.

Until you have learned from the past, you are destined to repeat it. Learning is a process of remembering and overcoming the past.

For a related message that will further clarify the situation, toss a coin three times:
3 Heads = 117   3 Tails = 18
1 Head and 2 Tails = 203   2 Heads and 1 Tail = 194

59
DHARMA

KARMA IS MAN'S PREDESTINED FATE AND DHARMA IS HIS RIGHT action. In a card game, karma is the hand you are dealt and dharma is how you decide to play the hand. You are not bound to a predetermined destiny, because you may play the hand well or poorly—your success or failure is up to you. The final outcome of your life develops from your learning, striving and skill, not just from what you were dealt.

Another way to look at dharma is as your duty to yourself and society. By following your self-nature you fulfill your purpose and increase the level of your awareness. Your karma conditions you through experience to create the character required to carry out your dharma. Of course, you always have the free will not to fulfill your dharma.

How does your question relate to your karmic need to fulfill your dharma? Meditate on this and ask for awareness in dreams.

For a related message that will further clarify the situation, toss a coin three times:

3 Heads = 174   3 Tails = 77

1 Head and 2 Tails = 202   2 Heads and 1 Tail = 14

60
CONTROLLING YOUR MIND

IN YOUR HEART YOU KNOW THE RIGHT THING TO DO AT EACH moment in time, but your mind wants to feel good right now. You go on a diet yet you want something sweet, so you eat a fancy dessert. Momentarily it feels good but the long-term result is fat. You get turned on sexually and have an affair that generates excitement in your life, but it might destroy your marriage.

Your mind will always choose immediate gratification at the expense of long-term satisfaction. Only the result immediately following the act matters as far as your mind is concerned. The second consequence doesn't matter. Your behavior is programmed by the initial reinforcement (either positive or negative) and it will increase that behavior. Each time you give in to what your mind wants, the more likely you will give in again.

When you let your mind's desire for instant gratification control you, the mechanics of your life don't work. The only way to take control of your mind is to understand how it works against you. Then make agreements with yourself and have the integrity to keep them. You either get results in life or you create excuses to explain why your life doesn't work.

For a related message that will further clarify the situation, toss a coin three times:

3 Heads = 153   3 Tails = 79
1 Head and 2 Tails = 212   2 Heads and 1 Tail = 49

69

61
CHANGING OTHERS

THE PERSON YOU DESIRE TO CHANGE IS ACCEPTABLE AS IS; IT IS YOU who has the problem. Sometimes the only way to be responsible is to remove yourself from your immediate environment. But if you want to maintain your relationship, the only way to resolve the issue is to change your viewpoint. The problem stems from your reactions to what the other person says and does, it's not the person who makes you react. You are responding to your viewpoint that this individual should be different. You want someone to change and be the way you want that person to be.

You feel you can't help being upset, but you can stop being upset once you fully accept the futility of the upsets and stop reacting. Right now, you're playing the part of the victim and you still have expectations of change. But people don't change unless they really want to.

It's all right for others to be just the way they are and it's all right for you not to be affected. By changing your viewpoint, you can transform the way you experience this part of your life. If you're no longer affected by the problem, you no longer have a problem even though nothing about the situation has changed except your perspective.

For a related message that will further clarify the situation, toss a coin three times:

3 Heads = 225   3 Tails = 196
1 Head and 2 Tails = 166   2 Heads and 1 Tail = 19

62
SOAP OPERAS

WE ALL HAVE SOAP OPERAS, STORIES WE REPEAT IN ONE FORM OR another until we can verbalize them without thinking. They're tapes that we play at every opportunity.

Here are some examples: "I'm underpaid and unappreciated." "My astrology is messed up because my Aries doesn't line up with my lover's Capricorn." "I've got bad karma." "My husband never takes me anywhere." "My wife doesn't give me enough sex." "My husband always wants sex." "My wife doesn't understand me." "It's my lot in life—my parents never had any money, so I'll never have any money either."

Those close to you know your soap operas. They've heard them so often they could probably repeat them word for word, just as you could repeat theirs. What is your primary soap opera, your number one gripe or complaint? When does it get aired and who is your primary audience—your mate, your friends, co-workers, relatives, strangers, your kids?

It's time to realize that every time you repeat your soap opera to someone, you program your subconscious mind with more negativity. Every negative thought generates a cause and effect reaction assuring that you continue to experience this negativity in the future. Meditate upon how this self-destructive pattern relates to your question.

For a related message that will further clarify the situation, toss a coin three times:

3 Heads = 234   3 Tails = 206
1 Head and 2 Tails = 57   2 Heads and 1 Tail = 178

63
ACTION/REACTION

THE BUKKYO DENDO KYOKAI SAYS, "WHENEVER A PERSON expresses the thought of his mind in action, there is always a reaction that follows. If one abuses you, there is a temptation to answer in kind, or to be revenged. One should be on guard against this natural reaction. It is like spitting against the wind, it harms no one but oneself. It is like sweeping dust against the wind, it does not get rid of the dust but defiles oneself. Misfortune always dogs the steps of one who gives way to the desire for revenge.

"One should get rid of a selfish mind and replace it with a mind that is earnest to help others. An act to make another happy inspires the other to make still another happy, and so happiness is born from such an act. Thousands of candles can be lighted from a single candle, and the life of the candle will not be shortened. Happiness never decreases by being shared."

Because your question concerns a thought in action, carefully consider all the possible reactions. How will you be tempted to respond to others' reactions? How could you harm yourself? How can you make others happy in this regard? Meditate upon these things and an outcome for the greater good of all involved.

For a related message that will further clarify the situation, toss a coin three times:

3 Heads = 152   3 Tails = 7
1 Head and 2 Tails = 44   2 Heads and 1 Tail = 205

64
FEAR & RELATIONSHIPS

MOST OF WHAT PASSES FOR LOVE IS REALLY FEAR: JEALOUSY, POS-
sessiveness, envy, frustration, anxiety. That's not love. You
assume that you have to be "in love" to be in a relationship—
but for the vast majority of people, love has nothing to do
with it.

Understand that the more you resist each other, the more
intensely you become involved with each other. It may be negative involvement, but it is still involvement. As long as you
struggle against something, you are locked into it and perpetuate its influence on your life. When you fight with each other,
you think your partner cares about what you are doing or
saying—otherwise he wouldn't bother to react.

You need to explore how you are being served by this relationship. What is the fear that causes the conflict? What needs
do you both have that aren't being met? What are you both
doing to cause the disharmony? How can you both create more
harmony? What do you want to happen between the two of
you? (Not what you say you want to happen, but deep down
in your heart, what do you really want to happen?)

For a related message that will further clarify the situation, toss a
coin three times:

3 Heads = 34
1 Head and 2 Tails = 2

3 Tails = 143
2 Heads and 1 Tail = 244

65
TOTAL COMMITMENT

OSHO TELLS A STORY ABOUT THE DISCOVERY OF GOLD IN COLOrado. People rushed in from all over the world to try to strike it rich. A multimillionaire sold everything he had to buy an entire hill and finance an extensive operation that incorporated the latest mining technology. He worked hard for a long time without finding any gold. Then he began to panic, thinking he had squandered his fortune foolishly and would end up with nothing.

So he put the hill and mining operation up for sale, hoping to salvage something from his folly. His family questioned him, asking, "Who will buy it when they see that you've failed?"

But a buyer did appear, and only after the papers were signed and money delivered did the original owner ask, "Why did you buy this hill after I found nothing and it has nearly ruined me?"

The other man said, "No one can predict life. Maybe you didn't dig deep enough." A few weeks after the mine was back in operation they struck gold a foot beneath the original diggings. The previous owner visited the new owner to congratulate him on his good luck, but the new owner said, "It wasn't luck. You didn't give yourself totally to it. You gave up when you should have gone deeper."

Meditate upon how your ability to totally commit to your goals relates to your question.

For a related message that will further clarify the situation, toss a coin three times:

3 Heads = 120   3 Tails = 85
1 Head and 2 Tails = 158   2 Heads and 1 Tail = 46

66
TRANSFORMATION

YOU DESIRE TO TRANSFORM YOUR LIFE. TRANSFORMATION LITER-ally means to rise above or go beyond the limits ordinarily imposed by form. It is a means of housing a different essence in the same form. To change a peach into a pear wouldn't be transformation. But to turn a peach into a peach that tasted like a pear would be transformation. The world remains exactly the same as it was before to a person who has experienced transformation. The immediate circumstances of someone's existence, too, remain the same. What has changed is that person's viewpoint of those circumstances and the way this individual relates to the world. The circumstances haven't changed at all.

Transformation is assured by doing two things: 1. Accept karma as your philosophical basis of reality. With this under-standing you accept all is as it is supposed to be, although you have the power to change it. 2. Accept what is, is. This means to accept the things that you cannot change without resistance. It is your resistance to what is that causes your suffering.

The acceptance of these two things will result in a trans-formed attitude of conscious detachment. Negativity will flow through you without affecting you.

For a related message that will further clarify the situation, toss a coin three times:

3 Heads = 69   3 Tails = 15
1 Head and 2 Tails = 236   2 Heads and 1 Tail = 48

67
LIMITATIONS

YOU AND YOU ALONE HAVE GENERATED THE LIMITATIONS YOU ARE currently experiencing. All progress and growth appear to be blocked, and general weakness is the order of the day. It is important for you to recognize the denials and limitations and seek to understand the reasons for them. If old karmic debts are the root cause, be aware that wisdom erases karma. You will not be bound to old mistakes any longer than it takes to learn from them.

Opportunities to transcend the limitations will emerge soon if you are aware and recognize them. Do not hesitate when the time is right because it may be a long time before you have another chance to free yourself.

What constructive activities can you engage in while waiting for the cosmic forces to favor you again? How can you prepare for the challenges that will emerge when current conditions have given way to new opportunities? Meditate to gather your strength and be open to the unseen assistance of your guides and Masters.

For a related message that will further clarify the situation, toss a coin three times:

3 Heads = 229	3 Tails = 42
1 Head and 2 Tails = 141	2 Heads and 1 Tail = 27

68
SELFISHNESS

EVERYONE IS SELFISH. YOU ALWAYS ACT IN YOUR OWN SELF-INTER-
est. That may not be the way you want to be, but that is what
is.

Even in a situation where you sacrifice yourself for your
children, you are living up to your self-image of what a good
parent should be. You couldn't live with the belief that you're
a poor parent, so you really act for yourself. Why would you
help a friend? Maybe because you selfishly wanted to make
sure your friend will be there for you if you're ever in a similar
situation. If you risked your life to save a stranger, did you
want to live with the fact that you might have saved him and
were too cowardly to act? Contributing to charity is a way to
relieve the guilt of having more and also the fear of losing it.

Yes, you need to give to receive in this world, but don't
falsely assume selflessness to gain self-esteem because problems also arise from your expectations of approval and appreciation. Don't stop assisting others—stop playing the martyr and
fooling yourself about why you assist others. Your true self is
found when your false self is renounced. Accepting that you
always act in your own self-interest is part of renouncing your
false self.

For a related message that will further clarify the situation, toss a
coin three times:
3 Heads = 145   3 Tails = 103
1 Head and 2 Tails = 76   2 Heads and 1 Tail = 7

69
SELF-INTEREST

BE CAREFUL OF FOOLING YOURSELF AND ALLOWING OTHERS TO fool you when it comes to self-interest. There are three types of people to consider: 1. Self-actualized people who know they act only in their own self interest; 2. People who know they act in their own self-interest, but attempt to make you believe otherwise; 3. People who don't allow themselves to know their own truth and sincerely believe that other people's interests are put before their own.

Do business with the first type of person, one who acknowledges how the game of life is played. The second type is attempting to fool you. The third type fools himself and also attempts to fool you.

Anything you want that will add pleasure to your life—success, love, friendship, freedom, material items—will cost you in terms of time, energy, money, sacrifice, or any combination of these things. If you don't accept the cost in advance, you'll regret it when the bill comes due.

Ask yourself how this relates to your question. What is the real price you'll have to pay to get what you want?

For a related message that will further clarify the situation, toss a coin three times:

3 Heads = 225　　　　　　3 Tails = 90
1 Head and 2 Tails = 162　　2 Heads and 1 Tail = 17

70
TAKING THINGS
PERSONALLY

YOU OFTEN TAKE THINGS TOO PERSONALLY AND YOU GET UPSET when you don't need to. Recall the last time someone upset you. If you were a different person in the same position, wouldn't that person have acted the same way? Of course. That person would have related the same way to anyone who represented what you had in fact represented. So there's nothing personal in it. It's just what happened under the circumstances. To take it personally is foolish.

Since it is impossible to change other people, you might as well accept them as they are if you're going to continue the relationship. After all, it is also your right to be what you are without changing your ideas or behavior to satisfy someone else. We are all free human beings and must be respected for what we are, not for what someone else wants us to be. If your behavior makes someone else uncomfortable, that person has the right to leave. The same goes for you.

Meditate on how this relates to your question and how you can enjoy all the warmth and joy this relationship offers while detaching from the negativity.

For a related message that will further clarify the situation, toss a coin three times:

3 Heads = 18   3 Tails = 186
1 Head and 2 Tails = 55   2 Heads and 1 Tail = 129

71
GRATITUDE &
SELF-SACRIFICE

THE BUKKYO DENDO KYOKAI TELLS A STORY ABOUT A THICKET where a parrot once lived together with many other animals and birds: One day a fire started in the thicket from the friction of bamboos in a strong wind and the birds and animals were in frightened confusion. The parrot, feeling compassion for their fright and suffering, and wishing to repay the kindness he had received in the bamboo thicket where he had sheltered himself, tried to do all he could to save them. He dipped himself in a pond nearby and flew over the fire and shook off the drops of water to extinguish the fire. He repeated this diligently with a heart of compassion out of gratitude to the thicket.

This spirit of kindness and self-sacrifice was noticed by a heavenly god who came down from the sky and said, "You have a gallant mind, but what good do you expect to accomplish by a few drops of water against this great fire?" The parrot answered: "There is nothing that cannot be accomplished by the spirit of gratitude and self-sacrifice. I will try over and over again and then over in the next life." The great god was impressed by the parrot's spirit and together they extinguished the fire.

Meditate upon how compassion, the spirit of gratitude and self-sacrifice relate to your question and to your life in general.

For a related message that will further clarify the situation, toss a coin three times:

3 Heads = 144   3 Tails = 98
1 Head and 2 Tails = 90   2 Heads and 1 Tail = 35

72
HATE

WHEN PEOPLE HATE, THEY ALWAYS LOOK FOR ALLIES—THE LESS
justified the grievance, the more pressing the desire. The more
that person wrongs someone they hate, the more fuel they add
to their own hatred. This is how humans work. The one who
hates has to silence his guilty conscience, and he does this by
convincing himself and others that you really deserve punishment. He cannot feel indifference or pity for someone wronged;
he must hate and persecute or else leave the door open to self-
contempt. Hatred can give meaning to an empty life. Therefore, understand that your adversary is to be pitied.

If you are upset it is because you are allowing this person's
problem to trouble you. You can't change a hateful person,
but you can change how you react. When you let go of your
expectations of approval or control, you begin to let go of your
anger, resentment and blame. The ideal self-actualized response
is to allow the negativity to flow through you without affecting
you. Let it go and go on with your life.

Meditate upon how an adversary relates to your question
and how you can best rise above this situation through positive
thinking and positive action.

For a related message that will further clarify the situation, toss a
coin three times:

3 Heads = 121   3 Tails = 23
1 Head and 2 Tails = 138   2 Heads and 1 Tail = 241

73
ANSWERING HONESTLY

YOU NEED TO BECOME MORE ASSERTIVE IN THE EXPRESSION OF your own rights, wants, needs and feelings. It is your right to maintain self-respect by answering honestly—even if it hurts someone else—as long as you are being assertive as opposed to aggressive. Sadly, from childhood we learn to deal with our problems indirectly and often dishonestly. We repress our actual feelings at the expense of our self-respect and often our physical well-being.

If you are not standing up for your rights, the long-term result is going to be detrimental to your relationships, and mental and physical well-being. The individual who takes the initiative reduces anxiety and increases his inner sense of self-worth. What you do in life generates your self-esteem—the more you act in a manner you respect, the more you increase your self-esteem.

Assertion is commonly mistaken for aggression, but assertion is standing up for your basic rights. Aggression is forcefully violating the rights of another. There is no need or excuse for such behavior.

When do you need to be more assertive? Who do you need to stand up to? When are you going to begin?

For a related message that will further clarify the situation, toss a coin three times:

3 Heads = 195   3 Tails = 72
1 Head and 2 Tails = 95   2 Heads and 1 Tail = 130

74
DOMINANT DESIRE

A STRONGER EMOTION WILL ALWAYS DOMINATE A WEAKER ONE. Every idea you perceive serves as a catalyst for a manifestation, although all ideas are not expressed in reality. It doesn't matter which idea you consciously favor or even know to be desirable—the stronger emotion will nullify the weaker one. The stronger emotion, in turn, will begin to permeate all aspects of your activities.

Desire is the nucleus of creativity. Eastern scriptures say that God created the world because a great desire arose within Him—a desire to create, to manifest, to expand. Enlightenment is considered by many to be true desire, freed from all objects to become pure love and compassion.

Meditate upon your dominant desires. Sometimes we manifest things we really don't want because we think so much about them. Meditate upon your short-term and your long-term desires in regard to your relationships, family and friends, career, level of success, spirituality, growth, social consciousness, and all other aspects of your life. Are your dominant desires leading you in the direction of your goals?

For a related message that will further clarify the situation, toss a coin three times:

3 Heads = 240	3 Tails = 64
1 Head and 2 Tails = 31	2 Heads and 1 Tail = 179

75
PROTECTION

A LACK OF AWARENESS OF YOUR SITUATION IS THE CAUSE OF YOUR difficulties. But you will be safe and protected if you can go within and remain at peace with yourself, the world and everyone in it. You are tired of the complications and difficulties that are part of your life, but you need to stop and ask yourself what you are seeking. Realize that you have the power to view your difficulties as masked opportunities. What you are presently experiencing is simply an opportunity to learn how to successfully cope with life. The sooner you learn, the sooner you will free yourself from the effects.

You are your own protection on the stormy seas of life. Peace will return—not as the result of changing circumstances beyond your control—but by changing how you respond to these circumstances. Accept the things you cannot change and change the things you can. It is sometimes difficult to recognize the difference, but you can do it.

Yes, there are many things beyond your ability to change. But what you can't change you might as well accept. With that acceptance comes peace.

For a related message that will further clarify the situation, toss a coin three times:

3 Heads = 155   3 Tails = 134
1 Head and 2 Tails = 196   2 Heads and 1 Tail = 45

76
GROWTH

VAGUE TWINGES OF DISCONTENT HAVE BEEN NAGGING AT YOU. You want things to change but you're not ready to act. But you know there is no growth without discontent. Deep within your center at the level of your Higher Self, you also know what is best for you, and that is always to strive for more awareness. Never allow yourself to reach a level of self-satisfaction where there are no new challenges. For most of us there will be no new growth without the agitation of discontent. Carefully study what displeases you because that will tell you what you are about to leave behind and possibly point you in a new direction.

Meditate upon your dissatisfactions and their source. Too often we wait until a situation is beyond repair before we decide to do something about it. This results in discarded relationships and career positions that might have been salvaged if the people involved had acted earlier. You will be better served by deciding exactly what you want and then communicating those needs to the person who can do something about them.

For a related message that will further clarify the situation, toss a coin three times:

3 Heads = 160   3 Tails = 227
1 Head and 2 Tails = 195   2 Heads and 1 Tail = 3

77
RELEASING

LET GO OF ANYTHING THAT IS NO LONGER USEFUL AND PURPOSE-
ful, and do so without regrets or resentment. This includes
such things as an unhappy past, books, philosophy, clothing,
a belief, your life-style or a club membership. Experience the
pleasure of the moment. By releasing anything when it is no
longer useful, you free yourself to start another learning experience without being bound to the old.

When you let go of what no longer serves you, you open
the door to new adventures. But all too often we find security
in the familiar and fear stops us from proceeding. Nietzsche
framed the words "live dangerously" on his wall. He said it
hung there as a reminder that his fear was tremendous.

Meditate upon the aspects of your life you continue to wres-
tle with but no longer serve you. Consider letting go and flowing in your natural direction, and being free to explore any
future learning experiences you anticipate with joy.

For a related message that will further clarify the situation, toss a
coin three times:

3 Heads = 143   3 Tails = 60
1 Head and 2 Tails = 51   2 Heads and 1 Tail = 144

78
JUDGING YOURSELF & OTHERS

YOU MUST GIVE UP YOUR JUDGMENTS ABOUT YOURSELF AND OTHERS. We all have an ego-self that is always thinking and judging, as well as a natural self. Harmony between these aspects of our personality is possible only when the mind is quiet. Your best performance at work, in sports or in psychic perception occurs when your mind is quiet and you are not trying to do well. Your results are just from doing what you know how to do, naturally.

In Zen, this attitude is "muga," an awareness of action lacking the feeling that "I am doing it." You cease to calculate or dwell upon winning or losing. You simply do your best by responding to an inner direction which carries you effortlessly through the experience.

Being nonjudgmental does not mean ignoring faults or mistakes. You don't turn off your brain and stop deciding what works and what doesn't. Being nonjudgmental means observing things as they are without labeling them either good or bad. Instead, accept that errors are a part of learning. Then a speedy correction can follow. Meditate upon how being nonjudgmental relates to your question.

For a related message that will further clarify the situation, toss a coin three times:

3 Heads = 66

3 Tails = 107

1 Head and 2 Tails = 244

2 Heads and 1 Tail = 197

79
APPROPRIATE ORDER

THE BUKKYO DENDO KYOKAI TELLS A STORY CONCERNING A QUAR-
rel between the tail and the head of a snake as to which should
be in front. The tail said to the head: "You are always taking
the lead; it is not fair, you ought to let me lead sometimes."
The head answered: "It is the law of our nature that I should
be the head; I cannot change places with you."

The argument went on until one day when the tail fastened
itself to a tree and thus prevented the head from proceeding.
The head became tired with its struggle and the tail had its
own way. With no eyes leading it, the snake fell into a pit of
fire and perished.

In nature an appropriate order always exists and everything
has its own function. If this order is disturbed, the process is
interrupted and all will go to ruin.

Meditate upon how this story relates to your question and
seek to understand the appropriate order in your own life.

For a related message that will further clarify the situation, toss a
coin three times:

3 Heads = 27   3 Tails = 157
1 Head and 2 Tails = 229   2 Heads and 1 Tail = 195

80
REVOLUTION

To ATTAIN TRUE FREEDOM, YOU HAVE TO FREE YOURSELF FROM THE repressive aspects of society, religion and government, none of which really wants you to be free. Society wants you to wear its approved masks of dress and behavior. Religion expects you to believe and contribute as dictated, and each year the government seeks to gain greater control of your life. When you accept the expectations of others, you repress who you are, succumb to fear, and give away your freedom.

To begin your personal revolution, start freeing yourself from your past programming by deciding what you want, not what your mate, boss, society, religion, or government wants you to want. What is it that *you* want? Realize you have a divine right to experience aliveness and joy.

The ultimate revolution is freedom from yourself, by rising above the fears that keep you from becoming all you are capable of being. It is also the freedom from obsessions and addictions. Consider what Albert Einstein said; "The true value of a human being is determined primarily by the measure and the sense in which he has attained liberation from the self."

For a related message that will further clarify the situation, toss a coin three times:

3 Heads = 113   3 Tails = 226
1 Head and 2 Tails = 4   2 Heads and 1 Tail = 58

81
ON NOT CARING

IT IS YOUR RIGHT NOT TO CARE. AFTER ALL, LIFE IS FILLED WITH "You shoulds." You should improve yourself. You should care about the charity program. You should care about the ozone layer, civil liberties, recycling aluminum cans, banning nuclear power and your Aunt Martha's broken leg. Your mother is getting older and thinks you should be concerned about elderly people in general. The PTA thinks you should attend monthly meetings, and the FCC wants you to be concerned about violence on television.

Ask your mate, children, parents, in-laws and friends what they feel your priorities should be and you'll receive different answers from each of them. But no one else can relate to your position and know what is best for you.

If you "did" all the things you "should" you would have no time left for yourself or for anything else. It is your right to choose whether or not you accept any responsibility for others' problems. Don't shoulder all of their "shoulds" yourself. You, and you alone, decide what is worth caring about.

Meditate upon the pressures you are currently experiencing. They are affecting you more than you consciously realize. It is time to make some decisions and honestly express your own needs.

For a related message that will further clarify the situation, toss a coin three times:

3 Heads = 32   3 Tails = 116
1 Head and 2 Tails = 215   2 Heads and 1 Tail = 156

82
A ROBOT

YOU DON'T HAVE A MIND, YOU ARE ONE. THAT MEANS YOU ARE A machine—a robot. We all have computer buttons; when they get pushed, you become a robot and demonstrate your automatic responses. A robot has no choice in the way it reacts. It has wiring and circuits constructed so that when a button is pushed, it responds according to programming. But when you do this, your life does not work as well as it could.

You can't change what you don't recognize, but you can identify your automatic responses and learn to override them. It's time to stop going on "automatic" when someone or something pushes one of your buttons. Instead, explore what provokes this reaction: What causes you to become angry quickly? What embarrasses you? What irritates you about your lover? What bothers you in your career? What makes you fearful? Does what other people think about you control you?

These are just a few of the situations that generate knee-jerk reactions—irrational responses that are rarely in your best interests. These are merely old programming buttons, not genuine reactions to what is. Consider how you can become aware of your buttons, catch yourself and override them before acting as a robot.

For a related message that will further clarify the situation, toss a coin three times:

3 Heads = 109	3 Tails = 143
1 Head and 2 Tails = 8	2 Heads and 1 Tail = 191

83
SURVIVAL

RATHER THAN STANDING ON PRINCIPLE, FALLING BACK ON PRIDE, or needing to be right, you'd be better served by winning the game. But your subconscious mind, which is a memory bank and operates like a computer, has one primary goal: survival. It achieves that goal by comparing the present to the past. In essence, your computerlike inner-guidance system says it is all right for you to live your life just as you do.

You have survived so far and your guidance system knows you did so by following its programing. According to computer logic, the system has to be right. Of course you consciously know that you aren't always right, but your subconscious doesn't. It responds only to programming and though you get to be right, you lose the game. When you are challenged, you become indignant. Your button is pushed and you react quickly.

But you are reacting to subconscious logic, not what is. You will be better served by becoming consciously aware of your programming instead of unthinkingly following it. The strong are patient and you must hold back in your immediate inclination to respond quickly. Don't repress—just give yourself a few moments to override the programmed responses that do not relate to the situation. Then it's time to win the game.

For a related message that will further clarify the situation, toss a coin three times:

3 Heads = 14	3 Tails = 50
1 Head and 2 Tails = 130	2 Heads and 1 Tail = 155

84
MODERATION

BUDDHA SUGGESTED MODERATION IN ALL THINGS. AT THIS TIME the universe is acting to balance the extremes in your life. Rather than resisting its efforts, accept them and balance your own behavior and attitudes. Remove any radical excesses in dealing with the object of your question. Temper your thoughts, words and deeds.

Life creates tension between opposing forces and you are constantly balancing the various aspects of your reality, whether it be between pleasure and pain, success and failure, excitement and boredom or joy and sorrow. To immediately detach from the current situation, you can decide not to manipulate the outcome and avoid choosing. Sit back and simply observe what unfolds. The observer understands that he is not his emotional responses, and when emotions begin to surface, he says, "This emotion is not me. It's a fear response generated by my need to control or choose. I don't have to do either. I don't have to identify with this emotion."

Meditate upon your need for moderation and your potential to become a peaceful observer.

For a related message that will further clarify the situation, toss a coin three times:

3 Heads = 136   3 Tails = 188
1 Head and 2 Tails = 16   2 Heads and 1 Tail = 150

85
COMMUNICATION

THE PRIMARY CAUSE OF PROBLEMS BETWEEN PEOPLE IS A LACK OF communication. One person doesn't know how the other really feels because there has been no direct discussion of the subject. Both assume they know and have thus established distorted concepts and behaviors based upon their own inaccurate viewpoints.

Never count on the other person knowing anything you haven't directly communicated. Your mate may not show his or her emotional needs but would give anything to hear you say, "I love you." The fact that he or she doesn't hear those words could create doubts about the relationship, which leads to negative subconscious programming.

Meditate upon how your question relates to communicating with the people closest to you. What can you do to improve this communication?

For a related message that will further clarify the situation, toss a coin three times:

3 Heads = 180

3 Tails = 49

1 Head and 2 Tails = 87

2 Heads and 1 Tail = 233

86
EMPTY YOUR CUP

THE MOST FAMOUS ZEN STORY CONCERNS NANIN, A JAPANESE master. A university professor once visited him to inquire about Zen. Nanin served the man tea, pouring his visitor's cup full and continued pouring. The professor watched the overflow until he could not longer restrain himself. "It is full to overflowing. No more will go in!" he said.

Nanin replied, "Like this cup, you are full of your own opinions and speculations. How can I show you Zen unless you first empty your cup?"

Self-actualization is the process of deprogramming, not the acquiring of new knowledge. All your life you've been filled with misconceptions, invalid views, convictions, moralities and notions that are restricting your life. Until you begin to question these traps, they'll block you. Once you realize that nobody really cares what you think, and nobody will save you, you can let go of these silly assumptions and get on with living, realizing that the only meaning in your life is that which you create.

For a related message that will further clarify the situation, toss a coin three times:

3 Heads = 192	3 Tails = 65
1 Head and 2 Tails = 71	2 Heads and 1 Tail = 125

87
THE ESTABLISHMENT

IT MAY BE IN YOUR BEST INTEREST TO MINIMIZE YOUR DEPENDENCY upon the establishment—the government, big business and organized religions. All of these attempt to manipulate, control and enslave you mentally because they demand conformity. This conformity breeds repression and kills creativity, and their message is, "Wear the right suit, cut your hair our way, act according to our rules, and we'll accept you." But if you repress what you really are, you become a hypocrite, complying out of fear.

The establishment isn't very self-actualized. It wants you to believe that all the answers can be found outside yourself. Even churches want you to find your answers on the outside, through a preacher, priest or set of commandments. Is it any wonder the establishment is threatened by a philosophy that encourges you to find the answers within yourself?

The establishment doesn't exist for you—you exist to sustain it. Society needs your body to work and make money, buy products, pay taxes, and donate to its well-being. It needs your body but fears your soul. If your soul is free, you may reject the dictates of the establishment. Meditate upon how your question relates to these dictates.

For a related message that will further clarify the situation, toss a coin three times:

3 Heads = 187	3 Tails = 41
1 Head and 2 Tails = 161	2 Heads and 1 Tail = 36

88
PROPER EFFORT

THE BUKKYO DENDO KYOKAI TELLS A STORY ABOUT A WEALTHY but foolish man. Once he saw the beautiful three-storied house of another man and envied it. He made up his mind to have one built just like it, thinking he was just as wealthy as the other man. He called a carpenter and ordered him to build it. The carpenter consented and immediately began to construct the foundation, the first story, the second story, and then the third story. The wealthy man noticed all this with irritation and said: "I don't want a foundation or a first story or a second story; I just want the beautiful third story. Build it quickly."

A foolish man always thinks only of the result, and is impatient with the effort required to obtain them. However, good cannot be attained without proper effort, just as there can be no third story without the foundation and the first and second stories.

Explore your desire for results and your willingness to apply the proper effort to get what you want. Are you willing to structure a solid foundation? Do you have the necessary patience? Meditate upon these things as they relate to your question and your life.

For a related message that will further clarify the situation, toss a coin three times:

3 Heads = 172   3 Tails = 235
1 Head and 2 Tails = 3   2 Heads and 1 Tail = 149

89
PREPARATION

LIFE IS A SUM OF YOUR PREPARATION PROCESSES. EVERYTHING YOU have ever experienced has led up to the person you are now. You have experienced hard times and sadness uniquely your own. But these problems actually have contributed satisfaction to your life, because without problems to challenge you, no personal growth would be achieved. You would have no way to learn how to handle difficulties and become aware of your ability to make your life work.

All the positive, beautiful situations in your life have also been part of creating the person you are today. Every experience of loving and caring, warmth and joy has helped to form the person you are. All of these experiences have been preparing you; you have been incubating up until this very moment. You have a unique background, unique abilities, unique conditioning. The question is, what have you been preparing for?

Meditate upon what all of your lifetimes and all of your experiences have been preparing you for.

For a related message that will further clarify the situation, toss a coin three times:

3 Heads = 105   3 Tails = 151
1 Head and 2 Tails = 38   2 Heads and 1 Tail = 206

90
MASTERING
RELATIONSHIPS

IN AN IDEAL PRIMARY RELATIONSHIP, BOTH PARTNERS RECEIVE SPE-
cial nourishment from their union to help each other become
all they are capable of being:
1. LOVE: Each will love as the other wants to be loved. 2.
ACCEPTANCE: Treasure the other's uniqueness without
expectations of change. 3. COMMITMENT: Both totally commit to the relationship—physically, spiritually, emotionally and
financially. Withholding reflects undermining doubts. 4. SUP-
PORT: Encourage each other in ways that increase self-esteem.
5. DETACHMENT: Let the little things go. 6. COMMUNICA-
TION: Openly share yourself, discuss mutual needs and compromise on solutions. 7. LISTEN: Be willing to appreciate the
other's position even when you don't agree. 8. COMFORT: Be
friends as well as lovers. Let your union be a refuge of balance
and harmony. 9. TRANSCEND ANGER: Hostility arises only
from the expectation of having things your way. 10. TIME:
Share activities that serve as building blocks of a good relationship. 11. TRANSCEND BLAME: Resist this expression of self-
pity, which is incompatible with karma. 12. SPIRITUALITY:
Foster each other's spiritual growth.

Meditate upon how these tenets apply to your question and
how you can integrate them into your life.

For a related message that will further clarify the situation, toss a
coin three times:

3 Heads = 81   3 Tails = 213
1 Head and 2 Tails = 168   2 Heads and 1 Tail = 30

91
AWARENESS IS

ACCORDING TO HUMAN-POTENTIAL TEACHINGS, AWARENESS IS how much you allow yourself to know your own truth. According to some Eastern spiritual teachings, awareness is observation without condemnation, and awareness can bring understanding only through silent observation.

If you want to understand something, you must observe it without criticizing. You can't pursue it as pleasure or avoid it as non-pleasure. Become aware of your body and your thoughts. Get to know what goes on inside you. The actual phenomenon of observing will change your awareness and with practice you will maintain attention without tension, a relaxed watchfulness.

The next time you are upset, just observe yourself. While observing, *you* are not. But the moment you label the agitation as possessiveness, anger, prejudice or another emotion, you become the observer and the observed, and you will immediately modify the experience. You'll analyze it and remember it, but the result is a division between you and the experience. Without labeling, you avoid judgment and the desire for a particular result. Instead, you will glean awareness.

For a related message that will further clarify the situation, toss a coin three times:

3 Heads = 158   3 Tails = 193
1 Head and 2 Tails = 111   2 Heads and 1 Tail = 38

92
HIGHER SELF

YOUR HIGHER SELF IS THE COLLECTIVE AWARENESS OF ALL THAT has ever been, all that is, and all that can potentially be—the Oneness. When you successfully access your Higher Self, you have all knowledge at your mental fingertips. You have an awareness of your past lives and the present, as it relates to you or anyone else you care to psychically know. How could this be? Simply, you are accessing the totality—the entire energy gestalt named "God."

Meditate upon accessing your Higher Self. Deepen your altered state by vividly imagining yourself ascending higher and higher, walking up a stairway through the clouds, or flying up until you have transcended levels of consciousness and find yourself in this all-knowing level of mind. In the Higher Self you will feel balance and harmony and will be at peace with yourself, the world and everyone in it. Call out to your own spirit guides and Masters and ask them to assist you in attaining the awareness you seek in the form of visualizations, inner knowledge or through thought language. Ask your question as a thought and then listen for the answer returning in the form of a thought.

For a related message that will further clarify the situation, toss a coin three times:

3 Heads = 36   3 Tails = 39
1 Head and 2 Tails = 118 2 Heads and 1 Tail = 32

93
CYCLES

YOU ARE ENTERING THE BEGINNING OF A NEW CYCLE AFTER A period of stagnation. You might have thought that progress has been blocked on some levels of your life. But now as the old cycle ends, you probably want to rush forward and initiate your plans with purposeful actions. Be aware, though, that you are at the very beginning of this new cycle. All is well and everything will continue to improve if you only allow things to proceed at their own pace.

Each new cycle brings with it obstacles that you'll have to negotiate without resistance. Working through these complications will open the door to new relationships or new ways of viewing some of the important relationships in your life. Be wary of expecting too much because that will only frustrate you. Clarity of intent is critical here—if you vacillate on your direction or imagined advantages, you could miss the cycle as it swings into action. Make sure you surround yourself with the right people and remain true to your principles.

If you use this time correctly, with positive motives and desires, it will carry you farther than you can imagine.

For a related message that will further clarify the situation, toss a coin three times:

3 Heads = 108   3 Tails = 85
1 Head and 2 Tails = 184 2 Heads and 1 Tail = 200

94
OUTSIDE/INSIDE

MANY SEEKERS DRIFT FROM ONE ORGANIZATION TO ANOTHER, OR from one spiritual discipline to another, searching for enlightenment. Today some channel has the answer, tomorrow it will be a new guru. The more the seeker searches, the more frustrated he becomes, because he is looking outside himself for the answers.

You are a spiritual being. Beneath all your layers of subconscious fear programming exists an enlightened soul with total awareness. What you seek is already there. It's like digging a well—the water is already beneath you. All you have to do is remove the layers of dirt and rocks to make the water available. Similarly, you must remove the barrier between yourself and what you desire.

Granted, it's more challenging to pursue internal awareness than it is to have someone else offer you magical answers. But someone else's answers may not relate to you. Therefore, meditate and read everything you can, attend many kinds of spiritual gatherings (as long as they don't want you to join anything) and then decide what you need to change about yourself. You will be well-equipped to create your own reality using all the tools at your disposal.

For a related message that will further clarify the situation, toss a coin three times:

3 Heads = 115   3 Tails = 89
1 Head and 2 Tails = 6   2 Heads and 1 Tail = 220

95
SELF-DELUSION

YOU WILL EXPERIENCE MENTAL DISCOMFORT WHEN YOUR BELIEFS conflict or your actions don't agree with your beliefs. For example, you think smoking is bad for your health, but you continue to smoke. You believe extramarital affairs are morally wrong, but you continue to be involved with someone outside your marriage. You say you should be more patient with your children, but you continue to yell at them.

The Law of Dissonance says that when your beliefs and your actions are incompatible, you will attempt to reduce the resulting inconsistencies by changing either your actions or your beliefs. The smoker will either become an ex-smoker or will deny or rationalize the actual health threat. The adulterous spouse will either stop the behavior or rationalize it, maybe by saying, "What my spouse doesn't know won't cause hurt feelings, and with my needs fulfilled, I'm a better partner." The impatient parent either changes the impatient behavior or rationalizes the attitude by saying, "It's better for me to yell and release the anger than to repress it."

Are any of your actions incompatible with your beliefs, and if so, what can you do to harmoniously resolve the conflict?

For a related message that will further clarify the situation, toss a coin three times:
3 Heads = 61   3 Tails = 143
1 Head and 2 Tails = 148   2 Heads and 1 Tail = 238

96
KARMIC REWARD

KARMA IS A MULTILIFE DEBIT AND CREDIT SYSTEM OF TOTAL JUSTICE with a single purpose—to teach. You can look at the good things that happen to you as rewards and the bad things as punishment, but that implies a judgmental authority figure exists. In reality, you and you alone judge what you need to experience in order to learn the lessons that will raise your level of awareness or increase your vibrational rate. All lessons are actually tests.

Say you manage to become wealthy and famous. From one perspective this is a self-bestowed karmic reward because you wouldn't have it if you hadn't earned it. But it is also a test to see how you will use your money and fame. One person uses it only for self-indulgence while another uses it to serve the planet. You can easily guess who is more likely to attain wealth and fame in a future incarnation.

Other examples of karmic rewards might be to be born to loving parents, to be beautiful or handsome, to have a natural talent, to inherit wealth, to be raised in a safe neighborhood or to be provided a good education. Meditate upon your own karmic rewards and how you can better use them.

For a related message that will further clarify the situation, toss a coin three times:

3 Heads = 209   3 Tails = 147
1 Head and 2 Tails = 28   2 Heads and 1 Tail = 123

97
CARRYING A BURDEN

TWO ZEN MONKS WERE ONCE TRAVELING TOGETHER WHEN THEY came to a stream widened by recent rainfall. By the bank stood a beautiful young woman dressed in fine clothes. She obviously wanted to cross the water but was distressed at the prospect of ruining her finery. Without hesitation one of the monks offered to carry the young woman across the stream on his back. She gratefully accepted his kind offer. The monk helped to hoist her up on his back and without more ado carried her across and put her down on the dry ground.

The two monks then continued on their way, but the other monk started complaining. "It is not right to touch a woman, especially one so young and lovely. It is against our commandments to experience close contact. How could you go against the rules for monks?"

The monk who had carried the woman walked along silently for a few minutes before replying. Finally he said, "I set her down by the river, but you are still carrying her."

Meditate upon how this story relates to your question, and the unnecessary burdens you carry.

For a related message that will further clarify the situation, toss a coin three times:

3 Heads = 122

1 Head and 2 Tails = 79

3 Tails = 232

2 Heads and 1 Tail = 5

98
POSSESSIVENESS

WHO OR WHAT DO YOU FEEL POSSESSIVE ABOUT? YOUR MATE OR loved one? Your friend? Your home? Your car? Possessiveness is ownership, but no one really owns anyone else. In fact, possessiveness is a self-perpetuating form of insanity. The possessor needs to possess more—more money, more power, more people. Possessiveness is the ultimate expression of insecurity in people who will never have enough.

If the possessiveness is in regard to a person, the individual being possessed will always experience a dichotomy—feeling complimented on being valued by the possessor but also yearning to be free. Yet you only want possession because you feel something is missing. Even when you don't know what is lacking, you grasp harder to hold on to ensure that nothing else is lost.

What is the real fear behind your possessiveness? What needs do you have that are not being met? What do you do in regard to this possessiveness that causes disharmony? What immediate actions can you take to create more harmony?

For a related message that will further clarify the situation, toss a coin three times:

3 Heads = 211   3 Tails = 243
1 Head and 2 Tails = 63   2 Heads and 1 Tail = 142

99
REPRESSION/INDULGENCE

WE ARE ALL HERE ON EARTH TO LEARN TO LET GO OF FEAR AND TO learn how to express unconditional love. But repression is a fear we all experience. Even the masks you wear in your day-to-day life are evidence of repression. However, what you repress never goes away. It will always surface when you grow tired of resisting it. By generating disharmonious karma, repression is even worse than indulgence, providing you are not harming anyone else through your indulgence. Why? Because you eventually get tired of what you indulge in, or, as expressed by the poet William Blake, "The road to excess leads to the palace of wisdom."

Bhagwan Shree Rajneesh felt his followers would move past their sexual obsessions faster through indulging in them rather than repressing them. He knew that repressed sexual energy can become perverted or turn into anger. He encouraged people to explore their sexuality, saying, "It is God-given energy. That means there is something to be learned through the experience."

Esoteric metaphysics teaches that when you repress what you are, a vibrational energy is generated within your soul that will have to be expressed—if not in this life, then in the next.

How do repression and indulgence relate to your question?

For a related message that will further clarify the situation, toss a coin three times:

3 Heads = 164   3 Tails = 213
1 Head and 2 Tails = 113   2 Heads and 1 Tail = 136

100
MAYA/ILLUSION

SPIRITUAL SEEKERS ARE OFTEN TOLD THAT THE WORLD IS AN ILLU-
sion, but don't take this literally. It doesn't mean that trees or
mountains or cities are unreal—it means the world exists as
you interpret it. You see it through your eyes and relate to it
based upon your past programming. Your thoughts and perceptions about the world create the negative and the positive,
but these are both illusions. They are not "what is," because
your neighbor sees and experiences a different world, your
parents another and your lover yet another.

The Buddhists often call people magicians because their
dreams create their world. "Thoughts are things and they create" is a metaphysical axiom that is founded in this concept.
Some metaphysicians teach that the real world is God, but that
we are blocked from experiencing God because we create and
project our own viewpoints to such a degree that we live in
illusion.

Attempt to separate fact from fantasy and meditate upon
any illusions in your life that may be working against you.

For a related message that will further clarify the situation, toss a
coin three times:
3 Heads = 152   3 Tails = 42
1 Head and 2 Tails = 214   2 Heads and 1 Tail = 110

101
GOOD FORTUNE

THE POSITIVE POWERS OF THE UNIVERSE WILL FAVOR YOU IN REGARD to your question as long as what you want does not conflict with someone else's desires. You must be very careful to keep your goals in harmony with the universe and to remain modest in your victories. If your ego falls out of balance, it will upset everything else and all gains will be lost. You must explore the intent behind your desire.

At this time you have unseen support in dealing with worldly affairs and social matters. You can easily move into new circles, but be careful of the company you keep. You are affected and influenced by everyone who comes into the space of your aura, so associate only with positive people who will inspire and motivate you. Your close personal relationships will greatly benefit from this time of good fortune. Your creative projects will also be favored.

You have great resources and your timing is ideal. Be sensitive to this blessing and maintain balance and harmony in your life. Also, appreciate those on the other side who support your quest.

For a related message that will further clarify the situation, toss a coin three times:

3 Heads = 42   3 Tails = 148
1 Head and 2 Tails = 150   2 Heads and 1 Tail = 64

102
WHAT YOU RESIST
YOU BECOME

FROM THE KARMIC PERSPECTIVE OF REINCARNATION, WHAT YOU resist you become. We are here on the physical plane to fulfill our dharma, resolve our karma, and, in the process, raise our vibrational rate by acting positively, with love and compassion. Because all negativity is actually fear, you can simplify your purpose in life to its essence, by letting go of fear and expressing unconditional love.

Resistance is always fear based. For example, if you avoid or mistreat Arabs, punkers, gays, and foreigners, these groups represent fears you need to address within yourself. Maybe the fear can be simplified to your unwillingness to accept those who are different. But that which you resist, you become. Ideally, you learn through love and wisdom, but if you don't have enough love and wisdom, you can be taught by directly experiencing the consequences of your attitudes and actions.

Perhaps you'll have to reincarnate in A.D. 2075 as an Arab homosexual punker who migrates to another country and has trouble adapting. Meditate upon how this concept of resistance relates to your question.

For a related message that will further clarify the situation, toss a coin three times:

3 Heads = 199	3 Tails = 236
1 Head and 2 Tails =165	2 Heads and 1 Tail = 140

103
EMOTIONAL ACTIONS

PEOPLE USUALLY BASE THEIR ACTIONS ON EMOTIONS. THEY INVENT logical reasons to justify their actions to themselves and others, but these reasons are mere rationalizations that rarely have much to do with facts. We are tempted to ask "why," of ourselves as well as others. The reasons, however, don't matter, even if we could possibly know what they are. They're buried in your viewpoint, which is the result of all your past programming.

When you ask "why," or try to explain "why," you demonstrate your lack of awareness. You also give away your power and reduce your self-esteem. You simply do what you do because you do it—that's why. Other people do what they do because that's what they do. That's what is.

You need to distinguish between "why" questions intended to take away power and "why" questions intended to clarify. "Why didn't you call last week?" is an attempt to manipulate. "Why is it better to use no-lead gas in my car?" is posed to clarify.

Relate this awareness to your question and think back to the times you've acted on your emotions and then invented logical justifications for your deeds.

For a related message that will further clarify the situation, toss a coin three times:

3 Heads = 128   3 Tails = 149
1 Head and 2 Tails = 97   2 Heads and 1 Tail = 218

104
ROLE MODELS

AN EVALUATION OF YOUR ROLE MODELS WOULD HELP YOU TO BETTER understand your current situation. People often choose role models in their youth, and these selections are made with little conscious awareness about how much you imitate them. They could be someone in school, a family member, a sports star, movie star, singer or anyone you admire. The role models become your self-image. You go through life making small decisions as if they were not part of any master plan, as if all along you were responding to individual circumstances. The truth is that there was a master plan. You set it in motion when you chose your heroes.

John Foster Dulles said when we pick great heroes, "we are, in reality and largely unconsciously, making a standard of conduct for ourselves. The next step is for us to make our own lives into the kind of effort which we think our chosen heroes would applaud."

Think back to your teenage years. Who were your role models? How have your role models related to your life? Have they worked for you? How might your awareness of your role models affect your future? Could you pick new role models that would better serve you in the future?

For a related message that will further clarify the situation, toss a coin three times:

3 Heads = 158   3 Tails = 72
1 Head and 2 Tails = 148   2 Heads and 1 Tail = 54

105
TRUE TEACHING

THE BUKKYO DENDO KYOKAI TELLS A STORY ABOUT A YOUNG MAN named Sudhana who sought enlightenment. From a meditating monk he learned that the pure and peaceful mind had a miraculous power to purify and tranquilize other minds. From a woman of benevolent spirit, he saw that charity was the fruit of wisdom. He learned patience from a poor, physically imperfect woman; he learned a lesson of simple happiness from watching children playing in the street; and from some gentle and humble people, who never thought of wanting anything that anybody else wanted, he learned the secret of living at peace with all of the world. He was taught the secret of harmony from watching the blending of the elements of incense, and a lesson of thanksgiving from an arrangement of flowers.

One day, while passing through a forest, he took a rest under a noble tree and noticed a tiny seedling growing out of a fallen and decayed tree, and it demonstrated to him the uncertainty of life. Sunlight by day and the twinkling stars by night constantly refreshed his spirit. Thus Sudhana learned from his experiences that there was true teaching to be gained from everything he saw or heard.

Meditate upon how Sudhana's many lessons apply to your question and the things you need to learn.

For a related message that will further clarify the situation, toss a coin three times:

3 Heads = 156	3 Tails = 81
1 Head and 2 Tails = 37	2 Heads and 1 Tail = 238

106
CHANGING PERSONALITIES

YOUR PERSONALITY IS THE SUM TOTAL OF YOUR PAST PROGRAM-ming and consists of an interaction of three factors: traits, viewpoints and habits. None of these are inherited. They are acquired and thus are alterable.

Habits are simply repetitive actions, such as the way you drive to work or the way you dress in the morning.

Traits are distinguishing characteristics, such as always being untidy, or always being immaculately groomed.

Viewpoints are the way you look at what happens to you and your specific attitudes toward aspects of your life.

The desire to change your personality must come from within as a result of realizing what is and isn't working. What habits are negatively programming your reality? What personality traits are working against you? Which of your viewpoints are programming disharmony? Once you are clear about what you want to become, if you are willing to exert a little effort, you can create a new personality that is an expression of everything you desire to be.

Meditate upon how the limitations of your personality relate to your question and upon any changes that would assist you to fulfill your desires.

For a related message that will further clarify the situation, toss a coin three times:

3 Heads = 176   3 Tails = 210
1 Head and 2 Tails = 252   2 Heads and 1 Tail = 89

107
SELF-ACTUALIZED LOVE

IT IS YOUR RIGHT TO STRIVE FOR SELF-ACTUALIZATION IN ALL AREAS of your life. In a self-actualized love relationship your love cannot be diminished by anything the other person said or did because you will not allow negativity to register. Instead, it flows through you without affecting you as you realize that the actions of other people do not affect you. Only what you think about their actions affects you.

Any time you have been upset or emotionally disturbed it was because you had expectations of approval or control. But your self-actualized love is not dependent upon being loved. You give freely, without any expectation of return, and you allow total freedom to your mate, expecting no more than your lover can give. You love what the other is, never expecting them to change. You find joy in the other's happiness, rising above fear and beyond emotional problems.

Most of us are still striving for self-actualization, but it is a goal within the reach of all of us. Meditate upon how a self-actualized love relationship relates to your question.

For a related message that will further clarify the situation, toss a coin three times:

3 Heads = 234   3 Tails = 83
1 Head and 2 Tails = 87   2 Heads and 1 Tail = 147

108
FEARFUL CONFRONTATION

WHAT DO YOU FEAR DOING? IF YOU FEAR DOING SOMETHING AND have the courage to do it anyway, your mind will soon perform a flip-flop and you may even become addicted to doing it. Say you fear sky-diving but force yourself to do it. The excitement this experience generates releases beta-endorphins, internally manufactured chemicals resembling opium and quite addictive. Thus the more you sky-dive, the more you will want to sky-dive. This applies to any exciting, internally stimulating experience, such as downhill skiing, risky business ventures, sexual affairs, public speaking, meeting new people, or whatever you originally feared. Knowing how the mind works in response to fear, you can use the information to conquer that fear once and for all or to avoid a potentially addictive situation—whichever you decide is appropriate to your situation.

Courage is the willingness to be afraid and to act anyway. Meditate upon what it would mean to truly confront your fear.

For a related message that will further clarify the situation, toss a coin three times:

3 Heads = 189   3 Tails = 145
1 Head and 2 Tails = 111   2 Heads and 1 Tail = 69

109
INEXPERIENCE

YOUR CONFUSION REGARDING THE SITUATION YOU QUESTION results from inexperience. Although you normally resolve your conflicts and make wise decisions based upon your experience, in this case you truly need to seek wise counsel. No one can be expected to have all the answers. Don't put pride before your well-being, or you could easily lose the game.

First, decide exactly what you want and then find a counselor who is enlightened in the area you seek to understand. If the advice is not to your liking, consider that this may be due to your inexperience. After all, if you knew what to do you wouldn't have to consult another.

The purpose of everything you do is to learn, to resolve karma and to increase your level of awareness. The current situation is part of the soul growth you must attain to make the progress you desire. Be a good student. Derive all you can from the experience of your counselor, and be humble and receptive in your communications with those who are willing to help you.

For a related message that will further clarify the situation, toss a coin three times:

3 Heads = 146   3 Tails = 24
1 Head and 2 Tails = 114   2 Heads and 1 Tail = 205

110
ENVIRONMENT & BELIEFS

EVERYTHING THAT SURROUNDS YOU IS AN EXTENSION OF YOURSELF. Your mate, children, home, furniture, car, pets, office and level of success are all physical expressions of your belief system and attitudes. Your environment is an illustration of your core beliefs, expressing your self-image and cultural overview.

But what the mind has created, it can also change. Change begins with the acceptance of new beliefs because your beliefs generate your thoughts and emotions, which in turn create your experiences. If you aren't happy with your current life and want to change it, you must change your core beliefs— your deep beliefs about allowing yourself to succeed in your career, attain wealth, find a fulfilling love relationship or remain healthy.

Your disharmonious beliefs are like a cage that restricts your potential and thereby your life. If you want to escape from the cage, you must first recognize that it exists and that you are not free. You cannot change what you don't recognize. Sadly, most people are unaware that they exist in a prison of their own making.

Meditate upon what you can learn about yourself by examining your environment. Decide which beliefs are working against you and set yourself free.

For a related message that will further clarify the situation, toss a coin three times:

3 Heads = 20   3 Tails = 132
1 Head and 2 Tails = 188   2 Heads and 1 Tail = 11

111
WISDOM ERASES KARMA

MANY WHO ACCEPT METAPHYSICAL IDEAS BELIEVE THAT THE MAJOR events in their lives are predestined, and hence there is little need to be concerned about personal safety. They say, "I won't be in an auto accident unless it is destined, so why wear a safety belt?" Or, "If I'm destined to die of AIDS safe sex practices won't save me anyway, so why bother?"

But if a major accident or devastating disease is destined as a karmic balance, remember the tenet that wisdom erases karma. The purpose of karma is to teach. Consider the possibility that the needed lesson is to stop being so *reckless*. Perhaps it is time to learn about the value of life.

Then the wisdom required to erase the karma could simply be using a safety belt to save your life, or using safe sex practices to avoid contracting the HIV virus.

Are you being reckless in any area of your life? Recklessness, aliveness and challenge are different things. You can generate aliveness and create challenge in your life without being reckless. Meditate upon how the idea of wisdom erasing karma relates to your life.

For a related message that will further clarify the situation, toss a coin three times:

3 Heads = 142   3 Tails = 214
1 Head and 2 Tails = 10   2 Heads and 1 Tail = 68

112
THE LAW OF EXPERIENCE

NEW INFORMATION ENTERING YOUR MIND SUPERSEDES PREVIOUS information of a similar nature. Once a pathway has been established in your brain, the information it contains will remain unless or until new information overrides the old.

For example, while horseback riding, you fall off and hurt yourself. If that is the end of your equestrian experience, you have been programmed negatively. Instructors know this and always urge new riders to climb back on the horse immediately after falling off. You need fresh, new input to erase the trauma of the fall. This is an innate, organic process that does not require your conscious attention or active participation because the basic processes of the brain are in an endless state of growth and reorganization.

This awareness can be used in altered-state programming because your subconscious mind cannot tell the difference between a fantasy and a real event. If perhaps you suffer from a fear of crowds, go into meditation and vividly imagine yourself being perfectly relaxed while in a crowd. Your mind will accept this as reality and invoke the Law of Experience. After a few weeks or months, you will overcome the old fearful programming. How can you use this law in your life?

For a related message that will further clarify the situation, toss a coin three times:

3 Heads = 231

3 Tails = 192

1 Head and 2 Tails = 56

2 Heads and 1 Tail = 162

113
SEARCH FOR TRUTH

THE BUKKYO DENDO KYOKAI TELLS A STORY ABOUT A MAN WHO was pierced by a poisoned arrow. His relatives and friends got together to call a surgeon to have the arrow pulled out and the wound treated.

But the wounded man objected. "Wait a little," he said. "Before you pull it out, I want to know who shot this arrow. Was it a man or a woman? Was it someone of noble birth, or was it a peasant? What was the bow made of? Was it a long-bow that shot the arrow? Was it made of wood or bamboo? What was the bowstring made of? Was it made of fiber, or of gut? Was the arrow made of rattan or of reed? What feathers were used? Before you extract the arrow, I want to know all about these things."

What will happen before all this information can be secured, no doubt, is the poison will have time to circulate all through the system and the man may die. The first duty is to remove the arrow and prevent its poison from spreading.

Likewise, in the search for truth some questions are unimportant. Meditate upon how this story relates to your question.

For a related message that will further clarify the situation, toss a coin three times:

3 Heads = 217   3 Tails = 238
1 Head and 2 Tails = 196   2 Heads and 1 Tail = 45

114
CLARITY OF INTENT

THE PRIMARY REASON PEOPLE ARE NOT AS HAPPY OR FULFILLED AS they desire to be is that they do not know exactly what they want. Sometimes, even when they think they know what they want, they fool themselves because the object is desired for the wrong reasons. If this is "the first day of the rest of your life," ask yourself exactly what you want to do with it. Your subconscious mind can then assist you in manifesting your desires.

Everyone wants happiness, but what that usually means is that they want to end the unhappiness or conflict in their lives. That is certainly within their power, too, if they have clarity and are willing to act. But it's not the same thing. True happiness is found internally, not externally. It is generated by a healthy attitude toward what happens in your life, by pursuing meaningful goals and by believing in yourself.

Meditate upon the clarity of your intent regarding your primary relationship, friends and family, career and level of success, spirituality, civic service, and any other area that is important to you.

For a related message that will further clarify the situation, toss a coin three times:

3 Heads = 237   3 Tails = 150
1 Head and 2 Tails = 79   2 Heads and 1 Tail = 1

115
GOALS

YOU MUST HAVE GOALS OR A STRONG GENERAL DIRECTION IN order to take control of your life. When you don't plan a life direction, you are making a choice, but inaction is no choice! Your subconscious mind generates the events in your life. If your thinking has been negative, you can be assured of moving toward potentially negative events. Thoughts are things—they create circumstances by programming your subconscious mind.

If you don't have goals or lack clarity of intent, start exploring what you would really love to do—something so enjoyable that you'd be playing rather than working. Don't even be logical in your search. When you become clear about what you want, everything will fall into place. Once you have pledged this direction, things begin to happen almost magically, as if you were a magnet drawing into your experience whatever is necessary for manifestation. The key to success is to have great emotional desire and no indecisiveness at all. The greater your emotional desire, the more energy you will generate to fulfill the goal.

Explore your clarity of intent in regard to personal and professional goals.

For a related message that will further clarify the situation, toss a coin three times:

3 Heads = 92   3 Tails = 247
1 Head and 2 Tails = 146   2 Heads and 1 Tail = 29

116
MOVING MIND

A ZEN STORY DESCRIBES THREE MEN OBSERVING A FLAG FLUTTERING in the breeze:

One man says, "The flag is moving."

The second man says, "The wind is moving."

The third man says, "You are both wrong; it is your mind that is moving."

As you observe your life, be aware that your mind is moving, creating the illusion that your world exists as it does. Zen perceives all as a unity: life is a whole and you are simply part of it. Dualities such as you and me, materialism and spiritualism, right and wrong, success and failure, morality and immorality do not exist. In removing these dualities, nothing's left to worry about—all is perfect tranquility. However, to experience this peace you must detach from your illusions and recognize that what exists is only that which you experience. You can either experience reality as a hostile separateness or a tranquil oneness. It's up to you.

It is this detachment that allows some people to be perfectly tranquil in the midst of a noisy, crowded or chaotic environment. They go into themselves and are not touched. Consider how this awareness can serve you.

For a related message that will further clarify the situation, toss a coin three times:

3 Heads = 124   3 Tails = 220

1 Head and 2 Tails = 231   2 Heads and 1 Tail = 72

117
LIMITS

ALTHOUGH YOUR MIND HAS AN UNLIMITED POWER TO CREATE THE reality you desire, limits obviously do exist. You can't control the weather, or the seasons or the actions of other people. You can also exceed your own limits because you have only so much patience, awareness, money or business expertise to draw upon in your decision-making process.

You need to accept your limitations as they now exist. This doesn't mean your position won't change in the future, but until it does, you need to accept what is. Limit your monetary expenditures and establish a plan that will carry you through the current circumstances. Cut back on your commitments to others. Control your desire to influence others. Let caution replace any extravagant behavior relating to your question.

If you are patient for a little while you will avoid making mistakes and being overwhelmed by misleading possibilities that won't serve you in the long run. Use this time to get to know yourself and to plan how best to act when circumstances change.

For a related message that will further clarify the situation, toss a coin three times:

3 Heads = 175   3 Tails = 221
1 Head and 2 Tails = 49   2 Heads and 1 Tail = 151

118
TIME MANAGEMENT

THIS TIME-MANAGEMENT PREMISE CLAIMS THAT YOU GET 80 PER-
cent of your rewards in life from 20 percent of your efforts.
Usually the 20 percent is comprised of activities that relate to
your natural abilities, things you do well and enjoy. The 80
percent is usually made up of two things: responsibilities, or
things you have to handle, and busywork, or places to hide.

To double your results, simply spend 40 percent of your time
doing what you do well. This doesn't mean you ignore your
responsibilities. Instead, delegate them to someone whose natural abilities fit these tasks. What may be a boring, mundane
task to you may be divine inspiration to someone else. Or use
a little of your increasing abundance to hire someone to handle
the responsibilities you don't enjoy.

The 80/20 plan is risky. It may not work. Then again, it can
work phenomenally. The secret to successfully incorporating
this principle is to develop a plan based upon your natural
abilities. This generates the creative energy which invigorates
you. Your best option in life is always to do what you love to
do.

For a related message that will further clarify the situation, toss a
coin three times:

3 Heads = 178   3 Tails = 233
1 Head and 2 Tails = 25   2 Heads and 1 Tail = 78

119
WILL VERSUS IMAGINATION

IMAGINATION IS MORE POWERFUL THAN WILLPOWER. AS AN EXAMple, lay a two-by-four board flat on the floor and walk along it. You will find it easy to do. You imagine you can do it and thus you are able to do it. But consider how you might feel if the board were placed between two skyscrapers and you had to walk along it. You'd be fearful and imagine falling, and you probably would fall, regardless of how much willpower you exerted. The board did not change at all; only your viewpoint of the board changed.

Change begins with imagination, and imagination is the most powerful reprogramming technique. While in meditation imagine your life as you desire it to be. Create vivid mental movies, fantasies in which you feel and sense everything that is happening—your emotions and the reactions of others who are observing your victory or accomplishments. Visualize your objective as an already accomplished fact. This way your subconscious fully comprehends the goal and can begin to manipulate circumstances that will eventually bring the goal into manifestation.

For a related message that will further clarify the situation, toss a coin three times:

3 Heads = 178   3 Tails = 223
1 Head and 2 Tails = 25   2 Heads and 1 Tail = 78

120
SUBCONSCIOUS MIND

YOU ARE THE SUM TOTAL OF ALL YOUR EXPERIENCES FROM YOUR birth to the present moment. If you accept reincarnation, all of the experiences of your past lives are also included. These past experiences represent all of your programming, memories wholly retained in your subconscious memory banks. Thus, your subconscious mind has made you what you are today—your talents and abilities, problems and afflictions are the result of the intuitive guidance of your subconscious. It has been directing you and it will continue to direct you, often in opposition to your conscious desires.

Why? Because the subconscious has no reasoning power. It simply operates like a computer, functioning as the result of programming. Every thought programs the computer—you have to think something before you speak or act. Thus if you are thinking more negatively than positively, you are literally creating a negative reality. If you are not happy with the way it is, it is time to transform your thoughts.

Consider how much you think negatively. Start catching such thoughts and neutralizing them before they become programming data by purposely creating a positive thought about the person or situation that upset you.

For a related message that will further clarify the situation, toss a coin three times:

3 Heads = 235
1 Head and 2 Tails = 33

3 Tails = 43
2 Heads and 1 Tail = 160

121
THE WAYS OF PRACTICE

THE BUKKYO DENDO KYOKAI TEACHES THOSE WHO SEEK ENLIGHT-enment the three ways of practice that must be understood and followed:

1. Disciplines for practical behavior: Every man, whether he is a common man or a way-seeker, should follow the precepts for good behavior. He should control both his mind and body, guarding the gates of his five senses. He should be afraid of even a trifling evil and, from moment to moment, should endeavor to practice only good deeds.

2. Right concentration of mind: Get quickly away from greedy and evil desires as they arise and hold the mind pure and tranquil.

3. Wisdom: Perfectly understand and patiently accept that desire and resistance cause suffering. Peace is attained through enlightenment and by following the Noble Path—right view, right thought, right speech, right behavior, right livelihood, right effort, right mindfulness and right concentration.

Meditate upon how the three ways of practice relate to your question and how you can integrate this awareness into your life.

For a related message that will further clarify the situation, toss a coin three times:

3 Heads = 165	3 Tails = 139
1 Head and 2 Tails = 58	2 Heads and 1 Tail = 115

122
THREE PILLARS OF DHARMA

THE BUDDHIST'S THREE PILLARS OF DHARMA OFFERS A PATH FOR spiritual living:

1. Generosity: Not grasping nor clinging—nongreed. The karmic results of generosity are abundance and deep harmonious relationships with other people.

2. Moral restraint: Not killing; not stealing; not committing sexual misconduct, refraining from actions of sensuality which cause pain or harm to others; not using wrong speech, not only telling the truth, but avoiding a lot of useless and frivolous talk or gossip; not taking intoxicants which cloud the mind.

3. Meditation: Concentrating the mind to stay steady on an object without wavering and cultivating insight to see more clearly the process of things, the nature of dharma.

Consider how these three pillars relate to your question and to your life.

For a related message that will further clarify the situation, toss a coin three times:

3 Heads = 201   3 Tails = 138
1 Head and 2 Tails = 109   2 Heads and 1 Tail = 242

123
PAST CAUSE

THE SITUATION YOU ARE CURRENTLY EXPERIENCING IS KARMIC— resulting from a past cause. Every feeling that floods through your body and mind, everything you experience, is generated by an event or series of events from another time and place. The events may have transpired at an earlier time in your present life, or in a previous one.

If you don't want to go to a past-life therapist, you can learn to regress yourself in meditation or self-hypnosis. In an altered state call in your guides and Masters, and ask to go back to the cause of the situation you desire to know more about. Imagine yourself going through a tunnel or crossing a bridge into your past. Trust your mind as impressions begin to form as visualizations, thoughts, feelings or as an inner voice. With a little practice you'll find you can easily maneuver yourself through time and space. Tell yourself, "On the count of three I'm going to move forward a few weeks so I can learn the outcome of this situation."

When you've learned what you want to know count yourself awake with positive suggestions, including the suggestion to awaken remembering everything you have just experienced.

For a related message that will further clarify the situation, toss a coin three times:

3 Heads = 180   3 Tails = 27
1 Head and 2 Tails = 166   2 Heads and 1 Tail = 162

124
SYMPATHY/EMPATHY/
COMPASSION

IN A HUMAN-POTENTIAL STORY YOU ARE TOLD TO IMAGINE YOUR-self walking down a road by the sea when you come upon a drowning man. Because you don't know how to swim, you can deal with the problem in one of three ways:

1. Sympathy: You jump in the river and drown with him.

2. Empathy: You sit down and moan and cry about him drowning.

3. Compassion: You do something about it. Throw him a rope or run and find someone who knows how to swim.

Meditate upon how this relates to your question and how you are currently addressing this issue. Compassion is thera-peutic because it allows you to share your being, and you benefit through the act of helping others. If you know yourself, are yourself, and act according to your own inner light, then life becomes a sharing experience that transcends the ego. Strive to act without expectations of appreciation or gain.

For a related message that will further clarify the situation, toss a coin three times:

3 Heads = 43   3 Tails = 119
1 Head and 2 Tails = 210   2 Heads and 1 Tail = 72

125
PERCEPTION

USE YOUR POWERS OF PERCEPTION TO GIVE YOURSELF AN ADVANtage in the situation you question. As in the martial art of aikido, consider yielding to others in order to receive their power and to learn their direction. Then you can lead a corresponding effort to use their power to your benefit.

To yield you must open, give up all judgment, and go beyond objectivity. Become an observer by using your perceptive abilities to walk in the other person's shoes. With this awareness you can act accordingly, keeping in mind that when you act with intent you incur karma.

This is an ideal time to establish a rapport with others. By maintaining a viewpoint of unconditional love, your perceptions will remain clear and accurate. You can use this awareness to attain peace, balance, harmony, and justice.

The more you use your perceptive abilities in positive ways the more you round out and refine your own character. This gives you the ability to influence and lead others with vision, or to live a rich life with little interference from others.

For a related message that will further clarify the situation, toss a coin three times:

3 Heads = 97   3 Tails = 114
1 Head and 2 Tails = 52   2 Heads and 1 Tail = 201

126
ENERGY CANNOT DIE

ENERGY CANNOT DIE. SCIENTISTS HAVE PROVEN THIS BY ISOLATING the smallest molecule of energy in a sealed cloud chamber where nothing could get out and nothing could get in. The molecule was too small to be seen with the naked eye, but it could be monitored on ultra-high sensitive film. The scientists observed that the energy molecule had a size, weight, pattern, and speed, and it moved continually within the chamber until it eventually fell to the bottom, appearing to die. But soon the molecule was back, only it had a new size, weight, pattern, and speed.

Human beings are energy. You cannot die, nor can those you love. We can only transform or reincarnate into new potentials of exploration. Energy also cannot stand still. By its very nature it must move forward or backward. When you are excited and challenged about what you are doing, your energy moves forward and expands. When you are bored, depressed, or burned out, your energy moves backward, preparing for a change that will bring some kind of a transformation.

Meditate upon your own energy as it relates to your question. Is it moving forward or backward? Is it expanding or are you preparing for a change?

For a related message that will further clarify the situation, toss a coin three times:

3 Heads = 250   3 Tails = 66
1 Head and 2 Tails = 29   2 Heads and 1 Tail = 167

127
EXPERIENCE THE MOMENT

SOMETIMES YOU GET IN THE WAY OF EXPERIENCING YOUR LIFE. ALL you have is this moment, now. That's it. You can't touch the past or the future. All that exists is this moment and you often seem incapable of enjoying it.

Unless you can fully experience the moment, enjoying the experience for what it is, then you are not living your life. You are simply wandering through your fantasies and probably mixing in a good deal of anxiety as you tread along. See what a phenomenal difference it makes in the way you experience what you are doing. At your next meal, don't carry on a conversation while you eat. Simply eat—feel what it feels like to chew the food. Taste what the food really tastes like instead of gulping it down and rushing the next forkful into your mouth. You might experience eating for the first time in your life. The next time you make love don't fantasize about making love to someone else or recall some past episode. Instead, fully experience the moment for what it is.

Relate this idea to other areas of your life. You may find that you are *experiencing* your life for the first time. Remember that wisdom grows out of experience.

Wisdom erases Karma

For a related message that will further clarify the situation, toss a coin three times:

3 Heads = 233   3 Tails = 45
1 Head and 2 Tails = 118   2 Heads and 1 Tail = 99

128
CORE VALUES

You NEED TO EXPLORE YOUR CORE VALUES. THEY REPRESENT WHAT you stand for, they are an energy source. Then consider your values as they relate to your earthly purpose. Go into meditation and ask yourself what are your deepest personal values. In meditating you will probably perceive several different answers, but one should stand out above the others.

Next, seek an image or a symbol emerging to represent your primary value. The symbol can be anything, a person, object, animal, sound, or picture. Don't consciously attempt to form it. Let the image take shape and happen naturally, whether it be the yin/yang symbol for balance, a tree branch for growth, a spring for perseverance or a bird for the soaring power of man.

Allow your symbol to center you and serve as a constant reminder of your core values. Draw a picture of it, or somehow incorporate a graphic representation of this symbol into your life, placing it where you will see it regularly.

For a related message that will further clarify the situation, toss a coin three times:

3 Heads = 188	3 Tails = 10
1 Head and 2 Tails = 207	2 Heads and 1 Tail = 40

129
STRESS BUTTONS

STRESS RESULTS FROM YOUR PERCEPTION OF EVENTS—HOW YOU react to situations. What is stressful to you might not be stressful to someone else and vice versa. You weren't born with any more stress-prone genes than the next person. In the end, it all amounts to attitude.

Research has shown that busy executives who have less stressful lives than others have high self-esteem, think the world is worthwhile, believe they can influence events around them and tend to see change and problems as opportunities. These attitudes don't eliminate stress as much as they seem to defuse it.

Consider your stress buttons. What causes you to be agitated? What makes you angry? What frustrates you? When does that tension begin to creep in? Make a list of all the stresses in your life, and if the cause isn't apparent, attempt to find it. If you become stressful every time you have a report on deadline, maybe it goes back to a childhood incident. Your fourth-grade teacher reprimanded and embarrassed you, which programmed an automatic anxiety response you are still carrying. Sometimes just knowing the cause is enough to alleviate the effect. If not, use this knowledge for reprogramming.

For a related message that will further clarify the situation, toss a coin three times:

3 Heads = 100	3 Tails = 13
1 Head and 2 Tails = 184	2 Heads and 1 Tail = 140

130
ENVIRONMENTAL HARMONY

ENVIRONMENTAL HARMONY CAN BE DIVIDED INTO TWO CATEGO-
ries: people and places. First, as you become more self-actualized, you'll find yourself less willing to remain in an environment
of negativity and manipulation. Thus, self-actualized people
seek freeing, supportive and growth-encouraging relationships, not only with their mates, but with friends and associates as well. If you are self-actualized and currently involved
in the wrong kind of relationships, you will do everything
within your power to improve these situations. Love and wisdom can accomplish the seemingly impossible.

Environmental harmony in a place is simply seeking a location where you find more peace than anywhere else, a physical
environment that vibrationally resonates with you. It may be
where you are now, in an entirely different area or perhaps a
different country. You are only a value judgment away from
moving there now. If you're happier elsewhere, it will reflect
in all aspects of your life.

Consider how your question relates to environmental harmony, and what you can do about it.

For a related message that will further clarify the situation, toss a
coin three times:

3 Heads = 23   3 Tails = 114
1 Head and 2 Tails = 133   2 Heads and 1 Tail = 76

131
ENERGY

Do you have the energy for your new project or direction? If you do have the energy and are clear on your intent, half the battle is already won. If you don't have the energy there is little chance of winning; you'll soon lose interest and put the project behind you, losing self-esteem in the process.

You can direct your energy in any direction you desire. You can use it for anger, resistance, creativity, love or success. It is the same energy. Some people use all their energy resisting what is—they want their mate to be the way they want him or her to be, they want society to be the way they want it to be, and they have no energy left for creativity, love or success.

When your goal is a joyous challenge and you combine your mental, physical and spiritual energy, you project the ultimate focused energy.

Meditate upon how energy relates to your question and how you can enhance your energy in the area of your concern.

For a related message that will further clarify the situation, toss a coin three times:

3 Heads = 233   3 Tails = 127
1 Head and 2 Tails = 50   2 Heads and 1 Tail = 222

132
BEING CENTERED

To be centered means to be physically relaxed, emotionally calm, mentally focused and spiritually aware. Your center is your inner essence, your evolved level of awareness. Your personality is your outer essence that has been cultivated by society.

Recall a time in your life when you felt centered. Recall everything about the situation. How old you were, the location, how it happened, how you responded. Then let yourself bring that feeling back into your body. If there is an image that helps to focus upon the feeling, use it to focus the sensations. Enjoy the feeling.

Next, imagine yourself being in difficult situations that normally would upset you, but maintain the awareness of your center and experience yourself remaining peaceful and harmonious despite the undesirable circumstances.

Practice centering yourself—regular use of this meditation can assist you to rise above the effects of fear-based emotions.

For a related message that will further clarify the situation, toss a coin three times:

3 Heads = 183   3 Tails = 5
1 Head and 2 Tails = 191   2 Heads and 1 Tail = 176

145

133
RIGHTMINDEDNESS

IT IS IMPORTANT FOR YOU TO BE RIGHTMINDED IN DEALING WITH others in the near future. Forces at play will require you to exercise attention to detail if you hope to accomplish your desires. This isn't a time to grasp the brass ring. Rather, attend to day-to-day matters, preserve the status quo and be alert to everything that relates to your question.

You could be attempting to take on more than you are prepared to handle. If this is the case you may want to reconsider the situation, without being tempted by the potential gains. By viewing circumstances with rightmindedness, you will avoid the pitfalls.

Be equally conservative in all your relationships and let sincere, heartfelt emotional responses generate harmony. Pretentious or flamboyant behavior will certainly generate disharmony at this time. Adhere to established roles and express your true feelings with compassion and honesty. Humility may be a lesson you need to learn, so avoid any manifestation of pride or the forces may turn against you.

For a related message that will further clarify the situation, toss a coin three times:

3 Heads = 171   3 Tails = 232
1 Head and 2 Tails = 169   2 Heads and 1 Tail = 126

134
PERFECT BALANCE

YOUR KARMICLY-DIRECTED HIGHER MIND HAS SET UP A DEBIT AND credit system that assures perfect balance. If the balance does not take place in the near future, it will take place later in your life, or in a future life. Therefore, always be very careful not to do things that you'll have to punish yourself for. Karma is constantly in motion on every level of your body and mind, and every thought, act and deed creates or erases karma. If an act is preceded by intention, then karma occurs.

Pick up a rock and throw it into a small pond. You are the cause, the splash and the ripples are the effect. Your actions disturb the harmony of the pond and the ripples flow out and back, until the pond eventually returns to its original tranquil state.

Similarly, all your thoughts and actions disturb the balanced harmony of the universe. Everything you do creates vibrations that flow out and back upon you until, through your lifetimes, your karma is eventually balanced and you are harmonious once again.

Meditate upon how your intentional acts relate to your question. Could your desire in any way engender the necessity of punishing yourself to balance your karma?

For a related message that will further clarify the situation, toss a coin three times:

3 Heads = 66   3 Tails = 202
1 Head and 2 Tails = 7   2 Heads and 1 Tail = 1

135
DOING NOTHING

IN YOUR EXTREMELY BUSY LIFE YOU SELDOM LEAVE YOURSELF THE time to do nothing. Doing nothing does not mean to sit around and talk on the phone or lunch with friends—it means to sit back and allow yourself the luxury of an empty space. Think of it as a pause in music, which is an important part of the composition. Without it, the notes would be indistinguishable.

Nothing means "no thing," do no thing. Look at your life and consider adjustments and corrections. The goal of some meditation is nothingness—a level without emptiness or loneliness—a level of utter happiness transcending ego. Buddha described this nothingness as overflowing compassion.

When you consciously stop seeing and thinking, you often begin to see things as they are. You are freed from old prejudices and previously programmed conclusions, and allow the space for new insights to manifest. In this state of no thing and no thought you can see.

For a related message that will further clarify the situation, toss a coin three times:

3 Heads = 108
3 Tails = 183
1 Head and 2 Tails = 57
2 Heads and 1 Tail = 93

136
MASTERY

DO YOU WANT TO BE A MASTER IN YOUR FIELD? MASTERY, A MAT-
ter of going beyond your limits, first requires clarity of intent
about what you want to do. You must make sure your belief
system isn't blocking you. What do you think and feel about
existing masters in the field you desire to conquer? If you feel
any resentment, you cannot become a master because you cannot become what you resent. Next, make a commitment to
excellence. Then master your abilities in the area in which you
desire to excel. This of course is easier said than done—to
develop mastery in anything requires great expenditures of
time, energy, effort and, often, sacrifices.

Be unwilling to accept mediocrity. To a master, average is
unacceptable. Examine your life to find the people and things
that take away your power and promote your being average.
Consider how you can remove the people and activities in your
life that encourage averageness. Participate in activities that
foster growth, and surround yourself with happy, successful
people who support you in being all you are capable of being.
You have the power and ability to rise above being ordinary
by focusing upon your desires and continually correcting yourself as you advance toward your mastery.

For a related message that will further clarify the situation, toss a
coin three times:

3 Heads = 101   3 Tails = 215
1 Head and 2 Tails = 61   2 Heads and 1 Tail = 24

137
OPPORTUNITIES FOR ENLIGHTENMENT

THE BUKKYO DENDO KYOKAI TEACHES THAT THE OPPORTUNITIES for enlightenment are endless:

Once there was a man who was burning incense. He noticed that the fragrance was neither coming nor going; it neither appeared nor disappeared. This simple awareness led him to gain enlightenment.

Once there was a man who got a thorn stuck in his foot. He felt the sharp pain and the thought came to him that pain was only a reaction of the mind. From this incident a deeper thought followed that a mind may get out of hand if one fails to control it, or it may become pure if one succeeds. From these thoughts, enlightenment came to him.

There was another man who was very avaricious. One day he was thinking of his greedy mind when the thought came to him that greedy thoughts were but shavings and kindlings that wisdom could burn and consume. That thought was the beginning of his enlightenment.

Meditate upon how these stories relate to your own search for answers to your question.

For a related message that will further clarify the situation, toss a coin three times:

3 Heads = 200   3 Tails = 130
1 Head and 2 Tails =146   2 Heads and 1 Tail = 33

138
TIME

THE GREATEST RESOURCE YOU HAVE IS TIME—YOU EITHER SPEND time or you waste it. Spending time means using it constructively, profitably, and ideally in a way that is fulfilling to you. Spending time might be working toward your success, a dinner with good friends, or sitting and doing nothing. Wasted time is any time spent with people you don't enjoy. Time spent doing busywork without benefit is also wasted.

Time is the most precious thing you have. When you allow people to waste your time you let them steal your life. We all have the same 1,440 minutes per day, but this time is lost forever unless you invest it in your future—by acquiring knowledge, learning skills, making business contacts or enhancing your personal life.

You don't have to respond to the demands of others. Only your value judgments keep you spending your time the way you want. How you decide to spend time has everything to do with the quality of your life and the level of success you can expect to attain. Meditate upon any changes in the way you spend your time that would serve you.

For a related message that will further clarify the situation, toss a coin three times:

3 Heads = 237   3 Tails = 68
1 Head and 2 Tails = 144   2 Heads and 1 Tail = 224

139
FACING FEAR

IT IS BETTER TO FACE A FEARFUL SITUATION THAN IGNORE IT. YOU tend to put off emotional confrontations, although you know they are inevitable. But if you will accept the inevitability of these encounters, you can begin to visualize how you will face and deal with your fear. These images will eventually reduce your fear to its proper proportions.

Some metaphysical teachers contend that if you are fearful you don't fully understand the situation. Fear is created out of past experiences and anticipated failures—that which is unknown and not understood. Once you comprehend your fear, it will be gone.

Be very careful that you don't use fear as a justification for avoiding life. To do so generates subconscious programming and you could actually program yourself to fear losing your fear—to be afraid that giving it up will take something away from you. But of course it will. It will take away the conflict, anger, worries and all other fear-based emotions.

Meditate upon how avoiding a fearful emotional confrontation relates to your question and how your fear may relate back to past experiences or anticipated failures.

For a related message that will further clarify the situation, toss a coin three times:

3 Heads = 47   3 Tails = 172
1 Head and 2 Tails = 4   2 Heads and 1 Tail = 80

140
SUCCESS

WHAT IS SUCCESS TO YOU? FOR ONE PERSON IT'S WEALTH, FOR another it's career satisfaction or recognition, still others measure success by their personal freedom or their level of awareness. Ideally, true success is all of these things combined with loving relationships.

Many people think success is gained by learning a particular skill, or launching an idea, or by means of contacts in the field. But statistically, none of this is true. Ninety percent of success results from energy, enthusiasm, self-image and self-discipline.

First you must know exactly what you want. Mental energy is necessary to learn, calculate and remember. Physical energy is the key ingredient of renewal. Enthusiasm usually is generated by doing what you love to do, but a winner's self-image is probably the most powerful success factor of all. Act in ways that make you proud of yourself, and never do anything that lowers your self-image in any way. Self-discipline means self-determination and perseverance in action—how you direct your time, energy and resources to manifest your desires. It's the one thing common to all successful people.

For a related message that will further clarify the situation, toss a coin three times:

3 Heads = 119   3 Tails = 20
1 Head and 2 Tails = 142   2 Heads and 1 Tail = 208

141
ACCOMPLISHMENT

ONCE THINGS ARE SET IN ORDER AND GOALS ARE ACCOMPLISHED, people want to relax and experience the benefits of their efforts. But this may not really serve you. Historically, when a country has reached its peak, it begins to fragment and decline unless an opposing force keeps it vigilant. The same is true of individuals. The only way to avoid a decline is to create a new peak you wish to climb—a new challenge for you to master.

If the situation begins to deteriorate, don't attempt to maintain an illusion that all is as it should be. Such a delusion is dangerous and will open the door to chaos. Instead, face the facts and carefully plan your actions.

If your question relates to personal relationships you can transcend the situation if you are cautious and imaginative in creating more aliveness in your lives. If you are concerned about business and career, you could be dealing with a long-term tendency or will soon experience an important transition. Caution is the key, followed by dedication to self-responsibility.

For a related message that will further clarify the situation, toss a coin three times:

3 Heads = 214   3 Tails = 149
1 Head and 2 Tails = 201   2 Heads and 1 Tail = 20

142
EMOTIONAL PURPOSE

YOU WILL NEVER SUCCEED BEYOND THE SCOPE OF YOUR VISION because goals and vision are different things. Vision represents the final outcome. While your goal might be to establish a successful restaurant, your vision is to own a nationwide chain of restaurants.

Examine your visions as they relate to all areas of your life—your relationships, your career, your level of success and your creativity among others. Be aware that you need an emotional purpose for a large vision. An emotional purpose will keep you driving forward. The desire to send all your kids to Harvard is an emotional purpose. To prove your worth to all the people who used to laugh at you is an emotional purpose. To rebuild your grandfather's lost fortune is an emotional purpose. To enjoy the satisfaction of mastery is an emotional purpose. But to succeed so you can pay off the mortgage without a struggle is a practical purpose. To earn enough to buy a fancier car is a material purpose. When people focus on practical and material goals, they tend to run out of enthusiasm when the going gets rough and so reduce their desires instead of striving to fulfill them.

Consider the motivation behind your desires. Is there a way to create an emotional purpose to support your important visions?

For a related message that will further clarify the situation, toss a coin three times:

3 Heads = 197   3 Tails = 183
1 Head and 2 Tails = 202   2 Heads and 1 Tail = 74

143
MEANING

PSYCHIATRIST VICTOR FRANKL CLAIMED THAT YOU NEED TO KNOW who you are and then, if your life has meaning, everything else will fall into place. When forced to a Nazi death camp during World War II, Frankl took with him his only copy of a manuscript he had written. A camp guard took the book, tossed it in the mud and stomped on it. Frankl said, "At that moment I closed the door on my past. I had to focus upon what I had to look forward to."

In the death camps it was the will to live that got people through. They had to have something to look forward to, or someone to need them. In other words, they had to have meaning—a reason to live. Without meaning, prisoners curled up and died.

When your memories exceed your dreams you have trouble. You can't live in the past or in the future. All you have is the ever present now, but you cannot live without the meaningful challenges that generate aliveness. They are what carry you into the future. Instead of a tensionless state, you need the challenge of a worthy goal.

Meditate upon how the search for meaning relates to your question and upon your own challenges and goals.

For a related message that will further clarify the situation, toss a coin three times:

3 Heads = 240   3 Tails = 188
1 Head and 2 Tails = 194   2 Heads and 1 Tail = 67

144
LIFE IS A GAME

YOU NEED TO INCREASE YOUR SELF-DISCIPLINE IN ORDER TO TAKE charge of your life. Life is a game: Some people play it as a game of struggle, sickness, poverty, or simply being right all the time. Others play the game for happiness, success and abundant health. We each play a game we ourselves set up. If your game were not bringing you some kind of payoff, you'd stop playing.

It would serve you to explore any secret satisfaction you receive from not being fully in charge of your life. For example, if you feel like you are vicitimized, are you receiving some satisfaction from being a victim? If you are unsuccessful or inadequate is there some kind of benefit in it for you? For example: You get attention. People feel sorry for you. People help you out or take care of you. You are protected from blame.

The types of games are infinite: "I can't find the right relationship." "I can only attain a limited level of success." "My boss doesn't like me." "My relationship is miserable." "My friends are always making demands of me." Meditate on the games you are playing and how they are serving you.

For a related message that will further clarify the situation, toss a coin three times:

3 Heads = 21   3 Tails = 249
1 Head and 2 Tails = 207   2 Heads and 1 Tail = 125

145
SELF-DISCIPLINE

INCREASING YOUR SELF-DISCIPLINE IS A MATTER OF BUILDING THE strength not to give up. All too often we say, "to hell with it" because we don't have the strength to struggle with the issue at hand. Sometimes we don't come right out and say, "to hell with it," although subconsciously we do. We continue our futile efforts because we can't admit to ourselves that we lack the self-discipline to do what is necessary.

If your lack of self-discipline causes you mental suffering, you will be stuck with the pain unless you get stronger. You can build your strength by increasing your willpower and generating more self-esteem. Self-esteem is promoted by what you do in life—so do things that make you feel good about yourself. Build your willpower by practicing one-pointedness, focusing only upon what you are doing and to do one thing at a time until the task is completed.

Practice persistence by making a pact with yourself to see the situation through. Be courageous—which means recognizing your fear, but acting anyway. Organize yourself and the project at hand, take first things first and follow through one step at a time. Develop mastery through practice and be unwilling to settle for less.

For a related message that will further clarify the situation, toss a coin three times:

3 Heads = 116   3 Tails = 94
1 Head and 2 Tails = 223   2 Heads and 1 Tail = 193

146
SEEING CLEARLY

WHEN SOMETHING BECOMES POPULAR AND FASHIONABLE, IT IS often difficult to view it clearly. For example, Chinese women have had their feet bound for thousands of years, wearing shoes to stunt their growth because small feet were considered a symbol of beauty. The feet of aristocratic women were so small they could hardly walk without assistance. Peasant women could not afford small feet, as they needed to be able to walk and work. The women with normal-sized feet were considered ugly, vulgar and uncultured. They were to be pitied.

Although the wealthy women were thought to be smart and beautiful, they were cripples. Any wealthy woman who didn't conform to the practice was condemned as being crazy because it was the only way she could obtain a handsome husband and marry well. Only when the practice was finally abolished could the people see its stupidity.

Just because the masses accept a practice or belief doesn't mean it is rational. Society continues to accept ideas that are as mindless as the concept that miniature feet equal beauty. Relating this to your question, thoroughly evaluate your own needs before accepting the dictates of others.

For a related message that will further clarify the situation, toss a coin three times:

3 Heads = 170   3 Tails = 222
1 Head and 2 Tails = 92   2 Heads and 1 Tail = 131

147
PEACE OF MIND

CONFLICT RESULTS FROM WANTING SOMETHING YOUR WAY AND not getting it. The sure way to attain peace of mind is to be concerned only with joyful giving, without expectations, and to let go of attachment.

No one other than yourself can give you anything, advice or material goods, that will result in lasting peace and satisfaction. Peace of mind comes from viewpoint—how you view what you do and what happens in your life. You and you alone can choose to view life as a hostile separateness or a tranquil oneness.

Metaphysicians believe that peace is the door to the inner kingdom of God. From this moment on, throughout your day, stop and remember to experience peace. Breathe deeply and take a few moments to relax and feel peaceful. Ask yourself, "What at this moment is lacking?" The more you do this the more peaceful you will become. Look at the things in your life that create turmoil and consider how you can stop judging and blaming. Let go of your expectations of approval or control. Accept what is and detach from the negativity by letting it flow through you without affecting you.

For a related message that will further clarify the situation, toss a coin three times:

3 Heads = 220   3 Tails = 10
1 Head and 2 Tails = 205   2 Heads and 1 Tail = 163

148
BRAIN POWER

YOU ARE USING ONLY A SMALL PERCENTAGE OF YOUR BRAIN'S TOTAL capacity—at the most ten percent. Imagine the results of even a two or three percent increase! Your brain is elastic; it will continue to grow as long as it is challenged and stimulated. Like other parts of your body, your brain, if not stimulated, will atrophy. Therefore, the greater the use of your brain, the more sharp and efficient your mind will become.

Consider more mental stimulation to keep your mind limber and agile: Read to sharpen visualization and imagination skills; practice problem-solving skills in games such as puzzles, Scrabble or interactive computer games; enjoy hobbies that focus your spatial skills by manipulating three-dimensional objects, such as model-building, sculpting and painting.

You can also keep your brain mentally fit by keeping your body physically toned. Even moderate physical activity is accompanied by positive electrical and chemical changes. Brain studies involving physical exercise have shown significant improvements in intelligence, speed of performance, and learning as well as decreased depression and lowered anxiety. Memory, attention span and motivation were also positively affected.

For a related message that will further clarify the situation, toss a coin three times:

3 Heads = 26

3 Tails = 185

1 Head and 2 Tails = 226

2 Heads and 1 Tail = 109

149
BALANCE

BALANCE HARD WORK WITH PLAY. IF YOU ARE A HIGH ACHIEVER doing something you love to do, it is often hard to spend time away from your work, doing things such as exercising, sharing with your family, enjoying a hobby or even attending to your spiritual needs. But this balance is critical to your overall well-being. Maintaining your equilibrium must become a central priority.

If you allow yourself to fall out of balance, things will go wrong in the area you are not attending to. If you're ignoring your relationship for your career, you can count on having relationship problems, which then will indirectly affect your career. If you aren't eating and exercising properly, you'll probably get sick, which again will indirectly affect the other areas of your life.

Meditate upon your own need to balance your life. What areas are out of balance? What can you do to create balance? How will the balance serve you?

For a related message that will further clarify the situation, toss a coin three times:

3 Heads = 182   3 Tails = 117
1 Head and 2 Tails = 135   2 Heads and 1 Tail = 228

150
HIGHER PRINCIPLES

UNLESS YOU STOP WHAT YOU ARE DOING AND ALIGN YOUR actions with the flow of the universe, you will make mistakes. By balancing yourself through the application of higher principles, you can bring harmony into the situation you question, and end your difficulty or confusion. Balance will result from being non-judgmental and compassionate, and from letting go of expectations and blame. Give up any ulterior motives and personal desires for advancement and accept that you may have to follow an indirect path to attain your goals. Forget clever strategies and rely upon your higher principles to guide you now.

Universal Law is what is, and it does not necessarily align with the desires of man. Thus, even when acting in accordance with higher principles you may experience an unexpected turn of events. Once you adjust to such a situation, a new creativity will inspire you to turn your problems into opportunities. This should allow you to explore some surprising new areas that could serve you in the future.

For a related message that will further clarify the situation, toss a coin three times:
3 Heads = 139   3 Tails = 165
1 Head and 2 Tails = 106   2 Heads and 1 Tail = 70

151
HAPPINESS

WHEN YOU ARE HAPPY YOU ARE ALSO MORE LIKELY TO BE healthy—you have fewer physical ills, you age slower and live longer. If you stop to think about it, you'll realize that just about every decision you make is based on what you think will bring you more happiness. This might best be defined as a state of well being—one that is filled with positive feelings toward yourself and the world.

Among the most important ingredients of a happy life is to love yourself. High self-esteem is the cornerstone of happiness and mental health. Also, strive for a loving life because research shows that people who are in love are actually happier. In fact, a happy marriage is statistically the most important contributor to well-being. But if marriage is not a consideration, almost any kind of loving relationship will increase happiness. This can be with children, family, friends, pets or a small group with a purpose. Another important factor for happiness is a job you like because work defines and affirms a feeling of self in powerful ways. We also channel our anger and aggression into wrestling with work projects.

Meditate upon how happiness relates to your question and what you can do to create more satisfaction in regard to what you want.

For a related message that will further clarify the situation, toss a coin three times:

3 Heads = 139   3 Tails = 199
1 Head and 2 Tails = 245   2 Heads and 1 Tail = 82

152
BELIEFS

IT IS TIME TO RECOGNIZE AND CHANGE THE BELIEFS THAT ARE NOT working for you. Psychologists and brain/mind researchers agree that these beliefs are the basis of your reality. Your beliefs generate the thoughts and emotions that create all of your experiences. If you are not one hundred percent happy with your life and you want to change it, you must change your beliefs.

Your beliefs are not buried deep in your subconscious mind. They are part of your conscious awareness, but are probably unexamined because we don't often explore our beliefs. Your beliefs are also unexamined because you accepted them long ago as facts, although they are not really facts. You may feel it's a fact that rich people are dishonest, and nobody really finds happiness, and sex can only be so good. It's what you believe so it becomes truth to you.

In this case your truths are like walls, surrounding you and restricting your life. If you want to tear down the walls you must first recognize that you are not free. You can't change what you don't recognize.

For a related message that will further clarify the situation, toss a coin three times:

3 Heads = 242   3 Tails = 43
1 Head and 2 Tails = 132   2 Heads and 1 Tail = 112

153
AVOIDING

EXPLORE HOW YOU ARE BEING SERVED BY NOT DOING WHAT YOU need to do when you need to do it. Maybe you fear success or perhaps you fear failure. By avoiding the issue, you don't have to cope with either.

You might fear success because if you were really successful it would change your relationships with your mate, family and friends. Maybe success would dictate other changes you wouldn't like, such as an increase in expectations, demands and pressures. Success can also generate a fear of ultimate failure at some future time. Examine your potential gains and losses realistically, and decide what will and won't work for you.

Explore why you might be afraid of failure, of being overwhelmed or of finishing a job or project. These fears interact with each other and generate even greater fears and stresses. Avoiding all of this can keep you from being judged, but it also can put someone else in the position of doing it.

Try to understand what blocks your action—the hidden reasons why you procrastinate. Ask yourself what is the worst that could happen. A full awareness of your potential loss will clarify your anxiety. Then explore how you can reduce the likelihood of this undesirable event from occurring and thus increase your chances of winning in each situation.

For a related message that will further clarify the situation, toss a coin three times:

3 Heads = 198   3 Tails = 237
1 Head and 2 Tails = 245   2 Heads and 1 Tail = 63

154
EMOTIONS

A Zen story concerns an elder monk in a Japanese monastery. The young novices were in awe of this man, not because he was severe with them, but because nothing ever seemed to upset him. A few of the young men decided to test the monk by devising a plan to scare him.

Early one dark winter morning, it was the monk's duty to carry tea to the Founders Hall. The young men hid in the alcove of a long and winding corridor near the entrance to the hall. Just as the monk passed, they rushed out screaming like crazy men. Without faltering a step, the monk continued walking on quietly, carefully carrying the tea. When he arrived at his destination he set down the tray, covered the tea bowl so no dust could fall into it and then fell back against the wall and cried out in shock "Oh-oh-oh!"

A Zen Master relating this story said, "There is nothing wrong with emotions. Only one must not let them carry one away, or interfere with what one is doing."

Meditate upon how your own emotional responses and this story relate to your question.

For a related message that will further clarify the situation, toss a coin three times:

3 Heads = 88   3 Tails = 200
1 Head and 2 Tails = 163   2 Heads and 1 Tail = 257

155
GOALS & VALUES

IT IS TIME TO EXAMINE YOUR VALUES AND MAKE SURE THEY ARE compatible with your goals. If your values and goals are not compatible, problems are occurring because you are fighting yourself. For example, if your major career goal is to become the best traveling salesman in your company and your key value is your home and family, your goal and value are not compatible because your work will take you away from your home and family.

Consider these key value areas: your primary relationship, children, career, friends, spirituality, physical well-being, finances, creativity, intellectual growth, recreation activities, material possessions and community or service involvements.

Clarify your goals by examining your general career objectives as well as your strongest personal ones. You must have goals, plan a life direction, and make choices. If you do not choose, destiny makes your choices for you, which can have sad consequences.

For a related message that will further clarify the situation, toss a coin three times:

3 Heads = 84   3 Tails = 228
1 Head and 2 Tails = 219   2 Heads and 1 Tail = 66

156
TIME TO ACT

WHEN YOU MAKE A DECISION TO ACT, THE ACT REINFORCES THE motivating belief behind it. The reverse is also true every time you fail to act. One self-disciplined act naturally leads to another, then another, helping to free you from those beliefs and viewpoints that work against you.

If there is an area of your life that demands attention and you are not acting, you need to determine what you really want—not what you think you should want. Discover what is blocking you from getting what you want. The block could be one of three things: a subsconscious fear; a hidden benefit, meaning you feel somehow served by maintaining the status quo; or a totally unrealistic desire. Then decide what you are willing to pay in terms of time, money, effort or sacrifice to get what you want.

Now you can freely choose what to do. When you feel you have to do something don't play the victim. Be a responsible, powerful person. Don't wait for the ideal time and conditions to act—chances are there will never be a perfect time. Success comes to those who are bold enough to take risks, and every time you act it becomes easier to act again in the future.

For a related message that will further clarify the situation, toss a coin three times:

3 Heads = 211   3 Tails = 190
1 Head and 2 Tails = 181   2 Heads and 1 tail = 103

157
RELATIONSHIPS

EVERYONE WANTS TO HAVE A WARM, JOYFUL, FULFILLING RELA-
tionship in which shared experiences encourage mutual
growth. But many people in relationships would be thrilled
just to find themselves in a relationship that is not a source of
pain or anguish. Even when the relationship doesn't breed
conflict, the couple experiences jealousy, possessiveness, and
envy. Yet they talk of love.

Krishnamurti asks, "Can a possessive or envious mind love,
or is it protecting its own pleasure, and thus operating out of
the fear of losing?" Where there is fear there is always aggression, so many love relationships also include a great deal of
aggression.

Is it time to change how you view your relationship? What
kind of relationship do you desire to establish? Could you say
to your mate, "You're perfect just the way you are—is it working for you?" Until you can let go of expectations and view
your relationships from a perspective of acceptance, you will
continue to experience problems. Meditate on what you are
doing to cause disharmony. What can you do immediately to
create more harmony?

For a related message that will further clarify the situation, toss a
coin three times:

3 Heads = 43   3 Tails = 248
1 Head and 2 Tails = 209   2 Heads and 1 Tail = 160

158
SELF-TALK

YOUR SUBCONSCIOUS MIND IS PROGRAMMED BY YOUR THOUGHTS, so what you think is critically important. Self-actualized people generate positive mental talk that increases self-discipline and supports high self-esteem. When you think, "I've got to get started on that project," catch yourself and replace that thought with, "I can't wait to get started on that project." Or you think, "I should skip watching the TV movie and finish the presentation." Catch yourself and say instead, "I choose to skip TV and finish the presentation."

Use positive self-talk, always based on your free choice of what you need to do. This programming is accepted by your subconscious mind and it will be incorporated into your natural way of thinking.

If you decide to catch yourself every time you think negatively, it will become easy to set a positive self-talk pattern into motion. Just remember that each positive thought is a "success opportunity," and replace your negative thought. A positive visualization will add to the programming power. Start catching and replacing your negative thoughts from this moment on.

For a related message that will further clarify the situation, toss a coin three times:

3 Heads = 216   3 Tails = 198
1 Head and 2 Tails = 211   2 Heads and 1 Tail = 14

159
PROSPERITY

THE UNIVERSAL FORCES ARE NOW FAVORING A TIME OF PROSPERITY. This is an ideal time for transcending the old and welcoming the new—a time for inspired growth like the flowering of spring. Use this time to cultivate and sow the fertile ground. Plant the seeds of rich new beginnings that will blossom into a fulfilling new life.

Now you can confidently embrace social situations and make new contacts. Positive influences will be echoed in many ways that will help you to create a positive reality. You are also able to exert leadership and to organize your career plans.

Focus your inner harmony and reflect this sense of peace in your worldly actions. Any actions that relate to the welfare of others will be especially fortunate. You have a responsibility to use your positive energy in ways that will also serve the planet. As a result you will benefit in the joyous way you experience your life and your physical well-being will be served as well.

For a related message that will further clarify the situation, toss a coin three times:

3 Heads = 11   3 Tails = 124
1 Head and 2 Tails = 191   2 Heads and 1 Tail = 236

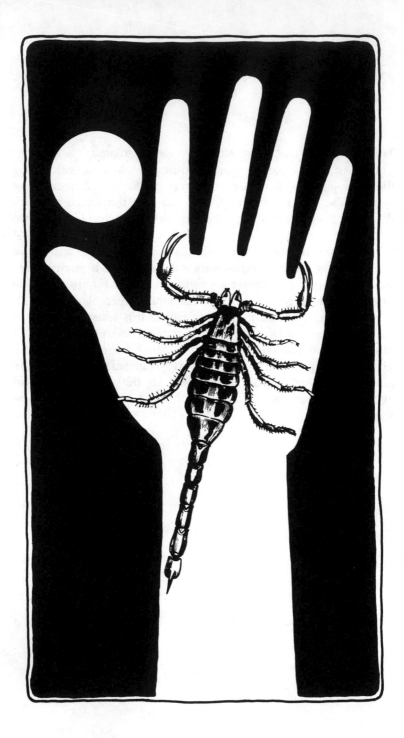

160
YOU ARE PERFECT

ON A HIGHER LEVEL OF MIND YOU ARE PERFECT—WHO YOU ARE IS perfect, even though what you do is not always perfect. For just a few moments, dwell only on your perfection. Silently in your mind repeat this affirmation over and over for a minute or two: "I know that who I am is perfect."

That's right. You are perfect. But is your ego-self challenging your perfection, saying, "What a dumb idea, I am not perfect." If so, this affirmation seriously threatens your ego. Your ego needs to remind you how unperfect you are because your ego prefers you to identify with your actions and to feel guilty about them. It wants you to judge, condemn and blame yourself and others.

You can neutralize your ego by loving yourself and your own perfection. Remember, in life you experience what you are deeply convinced is so. Meditate on loving yourself and accepting your perfection.

For a related message that will further clarify the situation, toss a coin three times:
3 Heads = 124   3 Tails = 163
1 Head and 2 Tails = 246   2 Heads and 1 Tail = 159

161
ADVANCE TIME

THE LONGER THE ADVANCE TIME YOU CAN INVEST IN YOUR SUC-
cess, the greater the payoff will be. All the extra energy and
effort will pay off down the line, if for no other reason than
that there is much less competition.

Most people are oriented to an immediate payoff. They can't
financially afford to wait, or they aren't emotionally capable of
being patient. It's estimated that only one person in ten will
put effort into anything unless the payoff is within a year's
time. It follows, then, that only one of the ten is emotionally
capable of investing time, energy, money, or sacrifice into
something that won't be profitable for five years or longer.

Meditate upon your willingness to invest the effort and
energy for a future playoff. Consider writing this simple
reminder and putting it in places where you'll see it regularly:
"I spend each moment doing the most productive thing I can."
Let this statement from you to yourself become your affirmation for success.

For a related message that will further clarify the situation, toss a
coin three times:

3 Heads = 245   3 Tails = 40
1 Head and 2 Tails = 140   2 Heads and 1 Tail = 103

162
ATTITUDE

You need to know that how you perceive a situation can be more important than what actually happens. When you interpret a situation and form an assumption, that assumption continues to influence you without your conscious knowledge.

Emotions such as fear, anger and guilt all affect the mind-body interaction, as do all other negative feelings. While fear and anger have evolved from basic survival instincts, guilt is wholly man-made—the result of judgments and evaluations based upon social customs, expectations and values. Nevertheless, you should always attempt to detach from all of these negative emotions.

Studies show that optimists tend to be less bothered by physical ailments than pessimists because optimists cope more efficiently with problems and experience less stress-related symptoms. Set a goal to reduce your stress and become more cheerful and optimistic about your life.

For a related message that will further clarify the situation, toss a coin three times:

3 Heads = 129   3 Tails = 220
1 Head and 2 Tails = 5   2 Heads and 1 Tail = 219

163
DESIRELESSNESS

A SUFI STORY TELLS OF A GREAT MYSTIC WHO LIVED SILENTLY AND alone until he was awakened one day by a messenger from God. The mystic rubbed his eyes and sat up to see the angelic presence standing before him.

"God is very happy with you," said the angel. "Your prayers have been heard and accepted. I am here to fulfill your desires. Just ask and they will be immediately fulfilled."

The mystic was a little confused. "You're a little late," he said. "There was a time when I needed many things, and I had many desires, but no longer. My desires are gone. I've accepted myself and I'm content. It no longer even matters to me if God exists or not. I continue to pray, but only because it feels good to me. I pray as I breathe. You come too late, I have no desires."

"But God has offered," said the angel. "I can't offend God by telling him this. Please, for my sake, ask for something."

"What do I have to ask for?" said the mystic. "I am happy and fulfilled. Nothing is lacking. Everything is perfect. But if you insist I ask, tell God I want to continue to remain without desire. Give me desirelessness."

Meditate upon how this story and the happiness attained by freedom from desire relates to your question.

For a related message that will further clarify the situation, toss a coin three times:

3 Heads = 54   3 Tails = 12
1 Head and 2 Tails = 207   2 Heads and 1 Tail = 129

164
GUILT

GUILT IS THE PRIMARY MANIPULATION PEOPLE USE TO ENTRAP ONE another, especially within families and other close relationships. There are only two reasons for someone to want you to feel guilty: either to control you or to hurt you. Neither is worthy of your consideration. Think about some of the common lines used to trigger guilt: "How can you treat me like this?"; "It was your fault that I was upset and didn't get enough sleep!"; "I've been waiting by the phone all week for you to call." But if you feel guilty, don't blame them—blame yourself for allowing someone to manipulate you.

There are three kinds of guilt: 1. Current Guilt, such as not spending enough time with the kids or not calling your parents as often as you think you should; 2. Long-standing Guilt, such as guilt over leaving your ex-mate, or guilt over refusing to allow your ailing father to move in; 3. Philosophical Guilt, such as not tithing to a church or giving to a worthwhile charity when you feel it is your responsibility.

After you've felt guilty long enough to balance the emotion with your actions, you can feel okay with yourself. But the common pattern is to repeat the guilt-inducing actions all over again, in a never-ending spiral. If you're going to do something about this most useless emotion, do it. If not, file it away, labeling it "experience," and get on with your life.

For a related message that will further clarify the situation, toss a coin three times:
3 Heads = 156   3 Tails = 34
1 Head and 2 Tails = 168   2 Heads and 1 Tail = 193

165
DEEP BREATHING

PRACTICE DEEP RHYTHMICAL BREATHING ONCE A DAY FOR SEVERAL minutes to bring fresh oxygen into your body. Doing this eliminates the carbon dioxide and other waste products in your system while strengthening and renewing your entire body.

Become aware of your breathing. Notice the frequency and depth of your breathing. Gradually increase the depth of your breaths as you slow the rate. Do this to the point where your breathing is the most relaxing and calming pattern for you. Focus on relaxing with each breath, and with each inhalation, breathe with greater calmness and peace. Let go of all tension in your body. See yourself inhaling energy, calmness and relaxation. Exhale the tension. Feel yourself blowing away the pressures and stresses of the day with every exhalation. Breathe in calmness. Breathe out stress and tension. Maintain this focused breathing for at least ten breaths.

Relax and rest your body at least half an hour each day. An ideal time is immediately after your deep breathing exercises. A quiet environment is essential; eliminate distractions and unnecessary noise. Make yourself comfortable and progressively relax your body. Regular relaxation gives your body a chance to recuperate and keeps its immune system strong.

For a related message that will further clarify the situation, toss a coin three times:

3 Heads = 95   3 Tails = 257
1 Head and 2 Tails = 211   2 Heads and 1 Tail = 57

166
BEING & BELONGING

ONE OF THE BEST WAYS TO INCREASE YOUR SELF-ESTEEM IS TO VALUE *being* more than *belonging*. This means that you value who you are and what is right and true for you more than you worry about being accepted by society and what other people think. This can earn you the label of a rebel and will often generate resistance from those whose self-esteem binds them to the dictates of society.

But don't take their negative input personally. If you feel criticized, or someone says something negative to you, don't take it as an attack on your self-worth. The idea is to begin transforming the way you experience your life. Realize that what someone else says or does, short of physical violence, does not affect you—only what you think about what they say or do affects you. Other people see you through their veil of old programming and you see them the same way. Neither side can be truly objective and accurately reflect the way things are.

Make it all right with yourself to let other people think they're right and not care. For a person with truly high self-esteem, being is more important than belonging.

For a related message that will further clarify the situation, toss a coin three times:

3 Heads = 184	3 Tails = 63
1 Head and 2 Tails = 39	2 Heads and 1 Tail = 7

167
COLLECTIVE POWER

YOU AND ALL THOSE CLOSE TO YOU CREATE A COLLECTIVE POWER. The universal forces are now synergizing this power and it can be manifested by a combined dedication and effort. This incredible energy can be tapped and used to your advantage if your desires are in accordance with Universal Law.

Be supportive and generous in uniting with others. You may have to do the organizing, for a strong leader will be necessary to maximize the power you can manifest. You will also have to be clear on your intent and possess an inner conviction as to the value of your goals. This will take exceptional awareness and dedication.

If you can perceive your role in the context of serving mankind, it will enable you to generate even more power. If your collective group is comprised of yourself and a lover or a large number of people, your united energy will help you to overcome all difficulties. If you always come back to your center for direction and inspiration and act with unconditional love, you will be assured of manifesting your desires.

For a related message that will further clarify the situation, toss a coin three times:

3 Heads = 15	3 Tails = 76
1 Head and 2 Tails = 104	2 Heads and 1 Tail = 222

168
ASK FOR WHAT YOU WANT

THERE ARE THREE BLOCKS THAT KEEP PEOPLE FROM ASKING FOR what they want: Fear, pride and low self-esteem. But if you want to get what you want in life you have to ask and keep asking. When you are rejected, keep on asking—never give up. The people who react negatively to your requests may simply need time to evaluate them and adjust their thinking. With the passage of sufficient time and repeated requests on your part, almost every "no" can be transformed into a "yes."

The key is learning to ask artfully. Getting what you want sometimes requires the courage to try a new direction when you don't seem to be getting what you need. Use cleverness and humor in your approach—it not only arouses curiosity, it also frequently overcomes resistance or opposition. A clever or imaginative request is often memorable, and can make more of an impression on others. Don't limit yourself to talking or writing, either. Try asking with more than just words—ask with your actions, too. Try different angles. Use your creativity and be flexible in making requests. If one approach doesn't work, you can always try another.

For a related message that will further clarify the situation, toss a coin three times:

3 Heads = 172   3 Tails = 54
1 Head and 2 Tails = 117   2 Heads and 1 Tail = 21

169
PERSONALIZING EVENTS

YOUR REACTIONS TO BAD NEWS SUCH AS MEDIA REPORTS OF DISAS-ters and crimes can lead to feelings of helplessness, lack of control and futility. Explore how you deal with such news. Try not to personalize the events. Instead, ask yourself whether you have any control over the situation. If the answer is "no," recognize that it is a random, coincidental event that has nothing to do with you. Be reasonably vigilant and accept that a certain amount of risk is part of being alive. Put the events in perspective by challenging any irrational beliefs.

Avoid doomsday thinking in which you project situations into a worst-case scenario, such as: "My child didn't come when I called—she's probably been kidnapped"; "My headache is probably a brain tumor"; or "If the Democrats get back in office they'll destroy the economy, everyone will be out of work and the bank will repossess our home."

You have the power and ability to control your mind and reject irrational thoughts before they build into fearful subconscious programming.

For a related message that will further clarify the situation, toss a coin three times:

3 Heads = 162

3 Tails = 128

1 Head and 2 Tails = 16

2 Heads and 1 Tail = 93

170
MADNESS & SILENCE

THERE IS A SUFI STORY ABOUT SOME TRAVELERS PASSING A MONAS-
tery to see people in catharsis. They were acting insane,
screaming and yelling, and pounding the ground. In their
midst was a Sufi master calmly observing the chaos.

"What a mad monastery," said the travelers. "The people
who came here to attain enlightenment have gone mad. Obviously the Master is too tired to deal with the situation."

A few months later the travelers passed the monastery
again, but now all the same people were sitting in silence, not
saying a word. A few months later they went by it again and
stopped to observe an empty monastery. The Master was sitting alone.

"Can you explain all this to us?" the travelers asked.

"When you passed by the first time you observed the begin-
ners, who were full of madness. I encouraged them to release
it. The second time you observed them, they had obtained
realization and calmed down. There was nothing else for me
to do, so I have sent them off. They can be silent anywhere
in the world. I am waiting for a new group. The next time you
pass there will be madness again."

Meditate upon your own madness that needs release and
how this story relates to your question.

For a related message that will further clarify the situation, toss a
coin three times:

3 Heads = 31   3 Tails = 140
1 Head and 2 Tails = 203   2 Heads and 1 Tail = 105

171
CREATIVE VISUALIZATION

USE CREATIVE VISUALIZATION TO SEE YOURSELF AS A HAPPY, healthy, whole person. The following are basic guidelines: Lie down, close your eyes and relax. Create and manipulate sensory impressions by imagining your reality as you want it to be. Transform your words and desires into positive visual images. Then deepen your relaxation and intensify your impressions. Add details, movement, depth, and style. Dwell upon the harmonious aspects of your life, both in the present and in the future.

Explore any resistance that may come up during the visualization session. Support your visualizations with positive affirmations in the present tense, such as, "I am self-accepting." "I now exercise regularly."

Practice visualization daily. In case of severe or life-threatening illness, practice visualization at least three to four times a day. Gear your sessions to specific images that assist your body to overcome illness. With daily practice, your images will become more vivid and clear. Like any growth process, visualization generates changes over a period of time.

For a related message that will further clarify the situation, toss a coin three times:

3 Heads = 182   3 Tails = 86
1 Head and 2 Tails = 50   2 Heads and 1 Tail = 244

172
SELF-IMAGE

YOUR SELF-IMAGE WAS CREATED BY A LIFETIME OF FEEDBACK FROM the world around you. Perhaps the most common problem people have with their self-images today has to do with the media and the culturally accepted norm. You are bombarded with ads, particularly on TV, showing beautiful people successfully getting what they want by using particular products or wearing specific clothes. Obviously, looking your best, having nice clothes and projecting a positive image is desirable. It's a good way to suggest to others that you feel good about yourself. But don't compare yourself to the people on the magazine covers and in TV commercials.

The right way for you to be attractive is to relax and be yourself. Express yourself—your unique qualities and enthusiasm for life and the people around you. Warmth, sensuality, sensitivity and humor have nothing to do with looks or clothing, money or fame. So forget the media images of what is appropriate and start to project the real you, the authentic you.

If you are not one hundred percent happy with the real you, know you have the power and ability to enhance who you really are.

For a related message that will further clarify the situation, toss a coin three times:

3 Heads = 173   3 Tails = 21
1 Head and 2 Tails = 102   2 Heads and 1 Tail = 131

173
PROJECTING CHARISMA

PROJECTING CHARISMA IS AN IMPORTANT PART OF COMMUNICAT-
ing with people. It involves projecting an inner warmth and
friendliness, acting self-assured and independent, exuding self-
confidence, being open and sensitive and allowing others to
know it, projecting assertive body language, and being secure
enough to let your vulnerability show. Remember, too, that
one of the most appealing human characteristics is the ability
to make other people feel at ease.

If your question relates to seeking new friends or a lover,
you must be prepared to create a relationship with a human
being, not a fantasy playmate. Your expectations must include
a willingness to accept someone as they are, not as you would
like them to be.

Consider what you have to offer: You have unique, positive
and interesting contributions to make in any relationship. We
are all unique and worthy of being liked as well as loved. But
unless you have a good sense of what you have to offer, you'll
probably have a hard time projecting it or communicating it to
someone else.

For a related message that will further clarify the situation, toss a
coin three times:

3 Heads = 158   3 Tails = 102
1 Head and 2 Tails = 242   2 Heads and 1 Tail = 71

174
FELLOWSHIP

THERE IS NO WAY TO LIVE OUTSIDE THE INFLUENCE OF SOCIETY, OR to avoid the effects of your community in the form of taxes, laws and the economy. No matter how independent you might like to be, you will always have to function to some extent within this environment, and your desires will relate to the needs of those around you. Society always functions best when every member is secure and contributes in his own way to the greater good.

The universal forces at this time are conducive to the accomplishment of social goals, but selfish interests will meet with more difficulty. This is a time of fellowship—a time to be consistent and principled in your actions and to be concerned with your fellow human beings as well as yourself.

With this in mind, now is also an excellent time for new endeavors, to create new structures, disciplines and directions for the unified attainment of group goals. This also relates to those you love—to your family and friends. It's not a time to seek as an individual. All your actions should also serve those who are closest to you.

For a related message that will further clarify the situation, toss a coin three times:

3 Heads = 168	3 Tails = 40
1 Head and 2 Tails = 1	2 Heads and 1 Tail = 215

175
SUBPERSONALITIES

IT IS TIME TO EXPLORE HOW YOUR SUBPERSONALITIES ARE AFFECT-ing your life. Within you lies the whiner and the critic, the manipulator and the martyr, the builder and destroyer, each with its own mythology—all coexisting as part of your personality. In meditation, you should begin by concentrating on one of your undesirable personality traits. Picture an image emerging to represent this part of you. It could be male or female, an animal, a monster, a symbol, or anything else. Let this image appear without attempting to consciously form it. Once the image has taken form, give it a chance to express itself without any interference or judgment. Have a mental conversation with it. Give it a name. Become aware of who or what causes this aspect of you to assert itself. Also, see if you can identify any fear associated with this subpersonality. Do this exercise over and over until you've discovered all of your undesirable subpersonalities.

In the future, the moment a subpersonality emerges, recognize it and observe it without judging or interfering. Then tell yourself, "This subpersonality is a part of me but it is not me." Your continual refusal to identify with the subpersonality can cause it to disappear.

For a related message that will further clarify the situation, toss a coin three times:

3 Heads = 166

1 Head and 2 Tails = 9

3 Tails = 212

2 Heads and 1 Tail = 87

176
COMPULSIVE THOUGHTS

IF YOU ARE BOTHERED BY FEARFUL OR COMPULSIVE THOUGHTS AND can't put them out of your mind, write them down and organize them into clear statements. Then you can create a plan to deal with each one of them. If a problem is real, you are capable of finding a real solution.

If your thoughts relate to ungrounded fears, you may want to explore the concept of thought stopping. Since every thought programs your subconscious mind, understand that positive begets positive, while negative begets negative. Always notice compulsive thoughts immediately and say these words to yourself, "Success Opportunity." Then, replace the negative thought with a positive one. If you catch yourself thinking, "I'll never get ahead with all these bills and responsibilities," stop and silently say, "Success Opportunity." Then think to yourself, "Every day in every way I move a little closer to financial independence." Then, visualize yourself having what you want as if it were already accomplished. This technique assures positive instead of negative subconscious programming.

For a related message that will further clarify the situation, toss a coin three times:

3 Heads = 174   3 Tails = 221
1 Head and 2 Tails = 52   2 Heads and 1 Tail = 107

177
THE FOUR ENERGIES

THERE ARE FOUR DIFFERENT KINDS OF ENERGY: MENTAL, EMO-
tional, physical, and spiritual. A balance is needed between
the four to keep them functioning in deep harmony, thereby
assuring you remain healthy and whole. Your mind, body and
spirit all respond to a shared rhythm of cooperation. An imbal-
ance in one area can rob you of energy in the other three, and
if your energies don't function in harmony, you will become
tired, unhealthy or ill because you are no longer whole.

You know there is a great difference between being physically tired and mentally tired. You also know that being emotionally drained is an entirely different experience. You probably
have experienced the importance of spiritual energy, too, as it
relates to your life purpose.

Meditate upon these four energy areas to see if you are in
balance. If not, explore what you can do to attain a balance.
Life's answers aren't difficult when you stop hiding from the
questions you need to ask yourself. You have all the answers
within you.

For a related message that will further clarify the situation, toss a
coin three times:

3 Heads = 197   3 Tails = 24
1 Head and 2 Tails = 8   2 Heads and 1 Tail = 238

178
HYPOCRISY

OSHO TELLS A STORY ABOUT A MAN WHO ARRIVED AT HIS LOCAL pub only to have a nun step out of the shadows and stop him before he could enter. "You must stop drinking before it's too late," she wailed. "This is the house of the devil. Repent your sins. Stop drinking."

The man thought for a moment and then said mischievously, "It isn't right for you to condemn something you've never experienced."

"I'm a nun. I can't drink," she replied.

The man talked to her for a while, persuading her to try just a little.

"But I can't enter a pub dressed as a nun," she said. "Why don't you bring some drink out to me in a coffee cup?"

So the man went into the pub, ordered his whiskey and asked for an extra shot in a coffee cup.

"Crisssake," exclaimed the barman. "Is that old nun hanging around outside again?"

Hypocrisy is pretending in one set of beliefs but practicing just the opposite. Meditate upon how his story relates to your question.

For a related message that will further clarify the situation, toss a coin three times:

3 Heads = 165   3 tails = 68
1 Head and 2 Tails = 45   2 Heads and 1 Tail = 179

179
THE POWER OF TRUTH

THE BUKKYO DENDO KYOKAI TELLS A STORY ABOUT A PRINCE WHO was skilled in the use of weapons. One day he was returning home from practicing and met a monster whose skin was invulnerable. The monster started for him, but nothing daunted the prince. He shot an arrow at him, which fell harmlessly. Next he threw his spear, which failed to penetrate its thick skin. Then he threw a bar and a javelin, but they failed to hurt the monster. Then he used his sword, but the sword broke. The prince attacked the monster with his fists and feet, but the monster clutched him in his giant arms and held him fast. The prince even tried to use his head as a weapon, but in vain.

The monster said, "It is useless for you to resist; I am going to devour you." But the prince answered, "You may think that I have used all my weapons and am helpless, but I still have one weapon left. If you devour me, I will destroy you from the inside of your stomach."

The courage of the prince disturbed the monster and he asked, "How can you do that?" The prince replied, "By the power of the Truth." Then the monster released him and begged for his instruction in the Truth.

Meditate upon how this story relates to your question.

For a related message that will further clarify the situation, toss a coin three times:

3 Heads = 154	3 Tails = 47
1 Head and 2 Tails = 241	2 Heads and 1 Tail = 184

180
EXPRESSING STRESS

YOU NEED TO IDENTIFY HOW YOU ARE EXPRESSING YOUR STRESS. Some primary signs of stress are: tension; continuous nervous activity; feeling incapable; excessive smoking, drinking or use of tranquilizers or other drugs; upset stomach; excessive sleeping; unfocused thinking; driving your car aggressively; turning every game into an intense competition; inability to sleep or frequent waking; loss of sexual interest; trying to do more than one thing at a time; easy irritability; high blood pressure; frequent headaches; cold hands; gritting your teeth; and over- or undereating.

Once you recognize the symptoms of stress, take a moment to mentally investigate every time you feel them. Ask yourself, "What would it take to eliminate the stress in this situation?" Then ask, "If I can't change the people or circumstances how can I change my viewpoint?"

You will resolve many of the problems in your life by accepting the unalterable realities (what is) and altering how you view what happens to you. You are never powerless. Meditate upon how this relates to your question.

For a related message that will further clarify the situation, toss a coin three times:

3 Heads = 124   3 Tails = 86
1 Head and 2 Tails = 221   2 Heads and 1 Tail = 199

181
SOCIAL HARMONY

SOCIETY REJOICES IN NEW IDEAS, INVENTIONS AND INNOVATIONS if they are in harmony with the desires of the community. But do not attempt to transcend established traditions if you seek approval and acceptance from the masses. All aspects of life must harmonize within the established laws and accepted patterns of mankind to have long-term success.

The universal forces are currently conducive to any harmonizing inspiration that will serve the greater good. These inspirations may relate to relationships, art, religion, education, healing, commerce, patriotism or similar areas. People need inspiration to encourage them to become all they are capable of being. It helps them understand universal perfection and truth.

The energy now available will cause you to be especially charismatic in communicating with others. Use it wisely, and in concert with your higher principles. Act confidently and your positive attitude will attract others of like mind who will want to cooperate with your endeavors.

For a related message that will further clarify the situation, toss a coin three times:

3 Heads = 163   3 Tails = 83
1 Head and 2 Tails = 52   2 Heads and 1 Tail = 171

182
BODY/MIND REACTION

THE FOLLOWING EXERCISE IS TO HELP YOU GET IN TOUCH WITH yourself. Sit back and relax, close your eyes, take a few deep breaths, and concentrate upon wanting to be somewhere else. Imagine yourself there. Experience the pleasure and joy you would feel if you were there now. Do this for at least two or three minutes before you read any further.

Now think about where the feeling manifested in your body. Some people will feel it in their face, others in their jaws, throat, stomach, arms, or legs. Wherever you felt the sensation is the way stressful reactions physically manifest in you. If you experienced tenseness in your jaws, the next time you find yourself wishing you could escape from your situation, you'll notice the tenseness in the same place. As a rule, any conflict not resolved at one level of organization must be handled at the next lower level. In life, unresolved intellectual problems must be dealt with by your body just as in business, unresolved administrative problems must be dealt with by employees.

When you don't deal with conflicting feelings your body is forced to deal with them. When you act honestly, expressing your real feelings, your body does not have to absorb the conflict. Consider how this relates to your question.

For a related message that will further clarify the situation, toss a coin three times:

3 Heads = 83   3 Tails = 169
1 Head and 2 Tails = 8   2 Heads and 1 Tail = 210

183
RESENTMENT

RESENTMENT IS RESISTANCE TO WHAT HAS HAPPENED—AN EMO-tional rehashing of an unalterable past event. The more you dwell upon it the more it programs your subconscious mind and the more it damages you. Like a computer, your subconscious mind works on the principle of garbage in and garbage out. Your mind will have to create circumstances to generate more negativity in the future, and it will prevent you from being as happy, healthy, or peaceful as you would be otherwise.

It doesn't matter if your resentment is justified or not, it will still damage you. It keeps you from seeing yourself as self-reliant, and it programs future failure. If you want your life to get better, you have to let go of your resentment.

You are not a victim. Karma dictated that you experienced exactly what you needed to experience to see if you'd learned from past mistakes. With resentment you give up control of your life and by blaming others, you give them the power to dictate how you feel, how you are programmed and how you act or react.

For a related message that will further clarify the situation, toss a coin three times:

3 Heads = 108   3 Tails = 197
1 Head and 2 Tails = 32   2 Heads and 1 Tail = 12

184
INITIATING/REACTING

TO INITIATE A CONVERSATION OR PROJECT IS RISKY—YOU DON'T know where it will lead or what will happen. You may fear your idea will be rejected or your plan may fail. Most people don't take much initiative in their lives. Rather, they live life at a minimal risk, waiting for others to take the initiative so they can react.

Unless you are willing to take the risk of acting first, you will live life with one foot in the safety zone. This limits your potential joy. By playing it safe, you can never enjoy life as an optimal experience.

Taking the initiative requires, but also generates, enthusiasm and energy. Maybe you won't win every time, but at least you become an active participant and know you gave your best. Your odds of winning are certainly better than for those who wait. When you're unafraid to initiate, you'll meet more adventurous people and open the door to challenge and aliveness. Take the risk. Go for the daring adventure. Be the one to initiate the meetings, ideas, projects, and proposals.

For a related message that will further clarify the situation, toss a coin three times:

3 Heads = 115

3 Tails = 46

1 Head and 2 Tails = 65

2 Heads and 1 Tail = 235

185
PREJUDICES

OSHO TELLS A STORY THAT DEMONSTRATES HOW PREJUDICES CAN function: A young boy and his father went to the zoo and stood in front of the lion cage fascinated with the animals inside. While the father was distracted for a moment, the boy inched between the bars of the outer crowd retainer and stood within inches of the cage. As a lion bounded toward the boy, the father leaped over the retainer and snatched his son to safety, just as the lion's claws shot out between the bars and swiped at the boy.

A journalist was in the crowd and he decided to write a short feature about it. Among other questions, he asked the father, "What political party do you belong to?"

"I'm a Nazi," the father replied.

The following morning's newspaper carried the headline, "A Dirty Nazi Steals the Lunch of a Hungry African Immigrant."

You can't trust your mind. Past programming has created prejudices that immediately mold facts into your viewpoint. Your understanding of an event is *your* understanding, but it isn't necessarily accurate or complete.

Meditate upon your own prejudices and how this story relates to your question.

For a related message that will further clarify the situation, toss a coin three times:

3 Heads = 48	3 Tails = 243
1 Head and 2 Tails = 112	2 Heads and 1 Tail = 180

186
COMBINING ENERGY

As a metaphysician, you understand that one and one do not necessarily make two when it comes to combining energy. The power of two like-minded people is multiplied many times, creating synergy as they work together to accomplish their goals. If you combine your energies with others for the greater good, there is no limit to what you can accomplish.

You and the person related to your question are vibrationally compatible, and your timing favors personal relationships. Examine your motives to make sure you are working together and not against each other, and that no one else will be hurt by your actions. You will be best served by pursuing a moderate course. It is not a time to indulge in excess, nor is it a time to make quick decisions. Much of what will transpire is karmic and beyond your control.

If the situation becomes stressful, do not respond with anxiety and fuel the fire. Instead let unconditional love guide your reactions—accepting what is, without judgment, without expectations and without blame.

For a related message that will further clarify the situation, toss a coin three times:

3 Heads = 120   3 Tails = 36
1 Head and 2 Tails = 61   2 Heads and 1 Tail = 179

187
LET GO AND LET GOD

YOU ATTEMPT TO MANIPULATE CIRCUMSTANCES JUST LIKE EVERY-one on this planet, but at times this will work against you rather than for you. Understand that whenever you try to control someone else you are expressing fear—fear that the other person isn't going to be what you want them to be or do what you want them to do. This is not your right.

It is time to let go and let God. Trust that to serve the greater good, you must open your hand and offer freedom. Become a living example of unconditional love by giving without expectation of return—by transcending your desire to judge and blame.

When you stop fighting life, life stops fighting you and transformation occurs. When you stop resisting the inevitable you can embrace it, accept it and rise above it. Letting go allows you to flow through life naturally, spontaneously, without restrictive preconceived ideas.

If you are open and willing to let go, if you can stop grasping for security, if you can trust in a higher power and in your own potential, a great adventure awaits you.

For a related message that will further clarify the situation, toss a coin three times:

3 Heads = 109   3 Tails = 249
1 Head and 2 Tails = 6   2 Heads and 1 Tail = 34

188
FOUR WAYS TO CHOOSE

THERE ARE FOUR DIFFERENT WAYS YOU CHOOSE WHAT YOU DO:

1. Denied choice: This is a victim's approach. You claim that fate and circumstance put you in the position of having no choice at all. You are dissatisfied and feel powerless.

2. False choice: This is "shoulding" on yourself. You respond to other people's expectations. But your performance only brings dissatisfaction and frustration.

3. Clear choice: This is a choice based upon what you want to do. Your actions fulfill you and only you.

4. Divine choice: This is a matter of doing only those things consistent with your purpose and who you are. You do the most appropriate thing at each moment in time. Divine choice springs from clear choice, but it disregards any selfish considerations. Although this is a more risky approach to choices, it offers the greatest potential for aliveness and joy.

Meditate upon how your question relates to these choices and how you will be best served in making your decision.

For a related message that will further clarify the situation, toss a coin three times:

3 Heads = 120   3 Tails = 76
1 Head and 2 Tails = 30   2 Heads and 1 Tail = 161

189
UNSEEN INFLUENCES

YOU ARE UNHAPPY WITH WHAT IS AND FRUSTRATED AT YOUR inability to create the reality you desire. But you must understand that unseen influences are at work. These include esoteric considerations such as past and parallel lifetimes, astrological factors, psychometric atmospheres, psychic attack or the influences of the moon. Mental and physical unseen influences include past programming, unrecognized altered states, the cumulative effects of diet and life-style, body somatotypes, brain-wave similarities, circadian body rhythms and positive and negative ions. And there are thousands more.

You can't change what you don't recognize, so you will be served by launching a four-step plan: 1. a physical examination to make sure you are healthy; 2. a healthy diet and exercise program; 3. a metphysical examination to explore the esoteric considerations, one you can do yourself if you have the awareness; 4. awareness expansion and regular mental reprogramming with meditation or self-hypnosis.

Meditate upon the importance of changing your life and your willingness to devote the time, effort and sacrifice necessary to do this. If it's important enough, you can do it.

For a related message that will further clarify the situation, toss a coin three times:

3 Heads = 239   3 Tails = 110
1 Head and 2 Tails = 58   2 Heads and 1 Tail = 99

190
TIME TO ACT

THINK IN TERMS OF WINTER ENDING AND A NEW PLANT EMERGING from the soil in a burst of creative activity. It is time to act and accomplish your goals. The universal forces currently favor the expression of your talents and abilities. This favorable energy will not last for long, so act quickly over the next three months.

Exactly what do you want? If it is a promotion, now is the time. If you desire to have a new idea accepted, present it now. If you want those in authority to be receptive to you, this is the moment to act. If you want a relationship to blossom and flower, you should be direct and honest in your communications with the one you love.

Dynamic inner growth awaits you if you choose to act. You will learn about your true self as a result of your choices. This self-realization will increase your self-esteem and give you confidence in the face of adversity. The future looks very bright if you are wise enough to act soon.

For a related message that will further clarify the situation, toss a coin three times:

3 Heads = 96

3 Tails = 71

1 Head and 2 Tails = 85

2 Heads and 1 Tail = 181

191
MANIFEST A MIRACLE

MIRACLES ARE ALL AROUND YOU, IF YOU TAKE THE TIME TO LOOK for them instead of rushing through life focused only upon your destination. Everything is an oracle—everything speaks to you if you are ready to listen. Insights on the answer you seek can be found in a newspaper headline, on a bumper sticker or in the shape of a cloud. The words of a child can crystalize your problems into clear observations. Maybe while walking down a path you notice a heart-shaped rock and pick it up. Can you see it as a message?

Expanded awareness is a small miracle that leads to larger miracles. The secret to manifestation is opening yourself to the miracles that await you. In meditation, ask your spirit guides and Masters to assist you. Begin to view life through spiritual eyes.

Miracles are yours for the asking. Ask and you shall receive. Let this be the first step to manifesting a miracle that will change your life.

For a related message that will further clarify the situation, toss a coin three times:

3 Heads = 91   3 Tails = 58
1 Head and 2 Tails = 207   2 Heads and 1 Tail = 77

192
HOW TO CREATE CHANGE

THERE ARE THREE WAYS TO CREATE CHANGE IN HUMAN BEINGS:
1. Add something to life, such as new people, things, environment or mental programming.
2. Subtract something, such as negative people, things, environment or mental programming.
3. Allow the individual to be his or her true self, instead of what any experiences have programmed this person to be.

You are already on the path of self-discovery. On a Higher-Self level you've made a decision to expand your awareness. Every day you learn a little more about who you are beneath your experiences. The secret to continued growth is to examine your fears because they keep you from knowing your True Self, thus preventing you from being all you are capable of being.

If you seek change in yourself or in someone else, know you can change yourself and accomplish all you desire. You cannot change someone else, but you don't need to. All is as it should be. It exists as a karmic challenge for you to conquer.

For a related message that will further clarify the situation, toss a coin three times:

3 Heads = 230	3 Tails = 25
1 Head and 2 Tails = 141	2 Heads and 1 Tail = 106

193
WHAT DO YOU WANT?

YOU ARE THE CENTER OF YOUR UNIVERSE. YOU ARE ALL-KNOWING and all-powerful, and all the answers you seek can be found in your Higher Mind.

Go into meditation and trust yourself. Ask yourself what you would like resolved in the near future. Then create a mental fantasy of the situation the way it is now. See it vividly in your mind. Now imagine it the way you want it to turn out. What do you have to know that you don't know to have it turn out this way? Are there realistic questions you need to ask yourself, or someone else? Are you willing to resolve this situation? If not, why not? What is the fear that is blocking you? If yes, decide how and when you are going to act.

When you act with intent, you create karma, so choose to act with unconditional love toward others. Ask yourself three questions: 1. If I get what I want will it result in a more honest, freer life? 2. If I get what I want will it improve the quality of my life? 3. If I get what I want will it help me to attain peace of mind?

For a related message that will further clarify the situation, toss a coin three times:

3 Heads = 9   3 Tails = 154
1 Head and 2 Tails = 51   2 Heads and 1 Tail = 86

194
CHAINS OF ATTACHMENT

A SUFI TEACHING STORY TELLS OF THE MAN WHO VISITED A GREAT mystic to find out how to let go of his chains of attachment and his prejudices. Instead of answering him directly, the mystic jumped to his feet and bolted to a nearby pillar, flung his arms around it, grasping the marble surface as he screamed, "Save me from this pillar! Save me from this pillar!"

The man who had asked the question could not believe what he saw. He thought the mystic was mad. The shouting soon brought a crowd of people. "Why are you doing that?" the man asked. "I came to you to ask a spiritual question because I thought you were wise, but obviously you're crazy. *You* are holding the pillar, the pillar is not holding you. You can simply let go."

The mystic let go of the pillar and said to the man, "If you can understand that, you have your answer. Your chains of attachment are not holding you, you are holding them. You can simply let go."

Meditate upon your own attachments and how this story relates to your question.

For a related message that will further clarify the situation, toss a coin three times:
3 Heads = 131   3 Tails = 214
1 Head and 2 Tails = 93   2 Heads and 1 Tail = 26

195
THE STRONG ARE PATIENT

PATIENCE MEANS HOLDING BACK IN YOUR INCLINATION TO EXPRESS your emotions when somebody upsets you or makes you angry, or when something causes you to become fearful. Don't repress or frustrate yourself. Just take a deep breath and go into a calm internal space and be patient long enough to logically consider your response.

Ask yourself: How do I respond in my best interest? Don't attempt to be right, don't act irrationally and don't say things you will regret later. The idea is to win the game. Consider nothing else.

The young martial arts student is taught to keep his mind like calm water because in the reflection he will perceive everything within striking range. The student also learns that anger muddies the water, increases his odds of losing and puts him at a distinct disadvantage because he can no longer think clearly.

Practice being patient when you are inclined to extreme emotions, such as anger, fear, adoration and anxiety. Connect your index finger and thumb in the circular "mudra" position as a reminder to be patient when you are tempted to act or speak too fast.

For a related message that will further clarify the situation, toss a coin three times:

3 Heads = 227   3 Tails = 100
1 Head and 2 Tails = 172   2 Heads and 1 Tail = 11

196
PSYCHIC ATTACK

THE MORE EMPATHIC YOU ARE THE MORE LIKELY YOU ARE TO BE affected by the thoughts of other people. If someone close to you thinks negatively of you, those thoughts can threaten your well-being. If there are several people thinking this way in one location, such as a family or work environment, then it's even more probable you'll be affected. Other people may not intentionally wish you ill, but their jealous or disapproving thoughts are projected and thereby produce an effect.

Classical psychic attack is the deliberate act of attacking another person by projecting negativity with mind control techniques and rituals. This can be accomplished by one person practicing black witchcraft or intensified by the work of a whole coven.

If you are being attacked purposely or unintentionally, the effects can range from nervousness and depression to physical illness. To resolve the problem, learn psychic protective techniques and refrain from all occult activities and reading. Spend a lot of time in the sun. Keep your psychic centers closed by eating well and often. Get involved in recreational activities. Seek to identify the source of the attack so you can exorcise any belongings that might relate to this individual.

For a related message that will further clarify the situation, toss a coin three times:

3 Heads = 216   3 Tails = 239
1 Head and 2 Tails = 12   2 Heads and 1 Tail = 195

197
BLOCKS

ARE YOU BLOCKING YOURSELF IN ANY AREA OF YOUR LIFE? ARE you hindering the establishment of a relationship or not allowing your union to be all it can be? Are you limiting your level of success? Are you denying your potential to communicate, or share, or love, or inspire? When you accept the fact you are blocking in a particular area of your life, attempt to locate the blockage in your body. All mental deadlocks are reflected in the physical body, and if you can pinpoint the location, you can begin to dissolve the impasse both mentally and physically.

You are body/mind/spirit, not body and mind and spirit. What your mind doesn't handle, your body will try to resolve, draining spiritual energy in the process. To rise above the effects, you have to work on your body and mind at the same time, and thus free yourself to harmonize with your spirit. In meditation, mentally draw down the universal light energy and imagine it flowing into your crown chakra of spirituality and down through your spinal column, cleansing and energizing your seven chakras—opening and charging the physical circuits.

You may also want to consider some of the energy balancing techniques, such as Reike, or manipulative physical therapies, such as rolfing, to achieve the balance necessary to become all you are capable of being.

For a related message that will further clarify the situation, toss a coin three times:

3 Heads = 237   3 Tails = 73
1 Head and 2 Tails = 185   2 Heads and 1 Tail = 209

198
WITHDRAWAL

A NATURAL PATTERN OF ADVANCE AND DECLINE EXISTS IN NATURE and in human affairs. With this in mind, you need to consider withdrawal as it relates to your question. But choose your timing wisely. You need to prepare properly before you act, and yet you must not wait too long or you could be trapped in an unworkable situation. This does not mean you abandon the situation. Rather, you may be able to realign the energy and change what is through a strategic withdrawal. Attempt to consciously detach from the emotions involved, withdrawing intellectually and emotionally so you can become mentally self-sufficient.

At this time it's impossible to win, and your own negative emotions will work against you if you decide to fight the situation head on. If there is discord in a relationship, attempt to view it as a growth phase and give up your unrealistic expectations. Explore any conflicts that exist between your ideals and current reality. Are your ideals realistic? Can you change your ideals without abandoning your higher principles?

For a related message that will further clarify the situation, toss a coin three times:

3 Heads = 124   3 Tails = 17
1 Head and 2 Tails = 92   2 Heads and 1 Tail = 111

215

199
LOVERS

LOVE IS THE MOST POWERFUL FORCE IN THE UNIVERSE. NEITHER time, birth, death, nor rebirth can ever separate those who have formed a deep mental, spiritual or physical bond. Once the soul's affinity has been established, those who know true love will always be "one."

Physical separation and parting for more than a short period of time, as we know it, is impossible. Mental separation is unknown on a subconscious level. Communication will always continue, although it may not be consciously perceived.

Lovers from the past will reincarnate within the same time frame again and again. Although they will not remember their past lives when they meet in their next life, they will be strongly attracted to each other and their love will be renewed. In each new incarnation the love will deepen; hopefully, it will grow more unselfish, until, after many lives, love is perfected.

People with whom you have a deep bond in this life have been close to you in a previous lifetime. You may have been lovers, friends or relatives in another time and another place.

Meditate upon how the positive force of love relates to your question. If your question relates to another person, meditate upon the potential of a shared reincarnational lineage.

For a related message that will further clarify the situation, toss a coin three times:

3 Heads = 168	3 Tails = 150
1 Head and 2 Tails = 219	2 Heads and 1 Tail = 56

200
LIKE ATTRACTS LIKE

PEOPLE CLAIM THEY WANT SUCCESS, BUT WHAT THEY REALLY WANT is the *results* of success. They do not necessarily want the responsibility that accompanies success nor do they want to pay the price in time, energy and sacrifice. They fail, or allow themselves to attain only a limited level of success because that is what they subconsciously desire.

Your thoughts are drawing to you that which you concentrate upon. The dominant thoughts will overwhelm lesser thoughts to manifeset a corresponding reality in the key areas of your life—your health, relationships, career and your financial and spiritual well-being. It is important to know what you want in all these areas. If you don't, you will attract confusion and all the undesirable effects that come along with it.

To get a general picture of how you've been thinking up until now, examine the state of your physical health, your primary relationship and the relationships you have with family and friends. Consider your level of career and financial success and your spiritual awareness. If one area is lacking, it is time to focus on your intent and change your thinking.

For a related message that will further clarify the situation, toss a coin three times:

3 Heads = 192   3 Tails = 39
1 Head and 2 Tails = 120   2 Heads and 1 Tail = 41

201
EXPECTATIONS &
FRUSTRATIONS

As YOU BECOME SELF-ACTUALIZED YOU LEARN TO LIVE WITHOUT expectations, which always result in frustrations and often lead to failure. You change jobs, change mates, change religions, change diets, all in the expectation that this one will work, this one will be successful and you'll be happy. But it is all futile until *you* change *yourself*.

An external expectation of success while you internally remain the same is a joke; it is an expectation destined for frustration and failure. Your world is a reflection of you—your perception picture—manifested. It started as an empty canvas, but your thoughts gave it form, color, composition, and meaning. You and you alone are responsible for it, and if you don't like the picture, it's up to you to paint a new one. You always have that power and that ability.

Meditate upon some of your recent expectations and how they worked out. What kind of internal changes would you have had to make for a more harmonious result? How would you like to repaint your life?

For a related message that will further clarify the situation, toss a coin three times:

3 Heads = 82   3 Tails = 123
1 Head and 2 Tails = 224   2 Heads and 1 Tail = 141

202
ACCEPT YOUR CHOICES

A ZEN STORY TELLS OF TWO MONKS WHO MET ON THE ROAD. AFTER their initial greetings, one monk asked the other, "What are you going to do tonight, my friend?"

The second monk replied, "I will meditate and pray in the temple. What are you going to do?"

"I'm going to spend a night of pleasure with the ladies," he answered.

The monks then went on their own ways, and that night in the house of pleasure, the monk was quite distracted. All he could think about was his friend meditating and praying. But was the other monk at peace with himself? No, he continued to think about his friend enjoying an evening with women.

When you make a choice, accept it completely and surrender to all the experiences that go along with your decision. When the choice is made, stop evaluating and let go of your desires and expectations. Experience what is.

Meditate upon how this relates to your choices and to your question.

For a related message that will further clarify the situation, toss a coin three times:

3 Heads = 254   3 Tails = 44
1 Head and 2 Tails = 78   2 Heads and 1 Tail = 190

203
PROBLEMS

LIFE IS A MATTER OF SETTING UP PROBLEMS AND RESOLVING THEM. This is true your entire life. Even your entertainment—books, television shows, movies—uses this device by establishing conflict and then resolving it.

The more aware you become, the more you'll flow with the stream of life instead of fighting against it. When you are fully aware, you'll discover that you are not really flowing along with the stream. Rather, you are the stream. It also follows that you are not a person trapped with problems, but are indeed the trap. And if you are the trap you've created your current situation to give yourself the opportunity to work it out. Problems make life interesting and give you something to do.

Meditate upon the idea of being the stream and being the trap and explore the aliveness that results. Look upon resolving the problems in your life from the playful perspective of solving a crossword puzzle or winning a game. Refuse to become fearful or overwhelmed. It is not necessary. You have the power and ability to work things out so that everyone wins.

For a related message that will further clarify the situation, toss a coin three times:

3 Heads = 58   3 Tails = 129
1 Head and 2 Tails = 167   2 Heads and 1 Tail = 224

204
INTEGRATION

EVEN THE MOST SELF-ACTUALIZED MAN CAN FEEL ANXIOUS, AFRAID or guilty, but he is not ashamed of feeling these emotions. He is not so detached from life that he ceases to feel. He simply feels the emotions without judging them, labeling them, or resisting them. He has no recrimination against himself for feeling them.

Condemning yourself or another cannot liberate—it can only oppress. You can never become whole by dividing yourself with inner conflict. Liberation begins with accepting yourself as you are and others as they are. That doesn't mean you can't change or get better. It doesn't mean you ignore mistakes. You simply acknowledge what is without making it worse and then you get on with your life. Acceptance is the foundation of all positive change.

Meditate upon how this relates to your question and your own need for integration in your life. Consider what you are worrying or feeling guilty about. How are you judging yourself? Can you let it go?

For a related message that will further clarify the situation, toss a coin three times:

3 Heads = 114　　　　　3 Tails = 64
1 Head and 2 Tails = 217　　2 Heads and 1 Tail = 190

205
BARRIERS TO FREEDOM

IF YOU ARE DOMINATED BY PASSIONS, WORRY ABOUT WHAT OTHER people think or are addicted to anything, you are not free. To attain freedom from the self you must rise above the effects of these things by learning to understand the nature of your own power.

Meditate upon the chains of illusion that keep you from being whoever and whatever you want to be and what you can do to break them. The chains exist because you created them, just as you have created your entire world of experience. You, the creator, are all powerful—magical. You can create heaven and hell, joy and misery, success and failure and you can stop creating them. You can stop weaving webs that trap you. You can decide to control passion, end addiction and let go of foolish fears.

While meditating, question how you are served by not allowing yourself to be the creator you really are. Is it too much responsibility to be all knowing and all powerful? What if you were to release your power and demonstrate what you can do?

For a related message that will further clarify the situation, toss a coin three times:

3 Heads = 122   3 Tails = 193
1 Head and 2 Tails = 142   2 Heads and 1 Tail = 80

206
FAMILY

THE CHINESE SAY, "BRING THE FAMILY TO ITS PROPER ORDER AND all social relationships will be correctly established."

Families share affection, loyalty, and faithfulness, and responsibility to one another. If the best aspects of family relationships could be integrated into business relationships, everyone would be served. The same would be true of social relationships.

In regard to your question, rely upon your inner awareness and natural affections to point your direction. If you desire the situation to resemble a family relationship, you must bow to authority and take the appropriate position. If you run into conflicts and are unwilling to defer, then the situation may become extremely difficult.

Attempt to clearly see and understand the organizational structure and how you best fit into it. What responsibilities are you willing to accept? What are you unwilling to do? Do not accept a role that doesn't suit your personality and abilities. Is there a way for the immediate needs of the entire family to be met?

For a related message that will further clarify the situation, toss a coin three times:

3 Heads = 240   3 Tails = 147
1 Head and 2 Tails = 85   2 Heads and 1 Tail = 30

207
COMPARISON

TO OBSERVE WHAT IS SOUNDS SIMPLE, BUT IT CAN BE VERY DIFFI-
cult. What is is an unalterable reality—something you have
no power to change. Your mind can't compare something to
something else to become aware of what is. It must let go of
the concept of opposites, allowing you to see what is instead
of what "should be."

You have been conditioned all your life to compare yourself
against others, against the hero or heroine, against the beautiful, handsome, brave or best. But it doesn't work, and you
need to stop doing it. When you compare yourself to someone
lesser in some way than you, it creates ego. If you compare
yourself to someone greater in someway than you, it can
depress you or make you bitter. Comparison also generates
unnecessary competition.

The idea is to accept yourself and others as they are. There
are some things you have the ability to change and some you
cannot. Accept what is without comparison. It will alleviate
you of many burdens.

For a related message that will further clarify the situation, toss a
coin three times:

3 Heads = 55   3 Tails = 106
1 Head and 2 Tails = 137   2 Heads and 1 Tail = 189

208
YOUR IDENTITY

YOU ARE WHOEVER SOMEONE ELSE THINKS YOU ARE. HOW COULD you be anything else? Their thoughts of you are their reality— their experience of you. If someone says something about you that isn't true, don't get upset. If they say something wonderful about you, don't take it seriously.

Whatever they say is what that person believes to be true about you. It is their truth. It many not agree with your truth, but that's all right. It will serve you to allow other people to view the world differently than you. No matter what someone else says or thinks about you, it does not change who or what you are. Your identity is always independent of other people's opinions.

Meditate upon the insecurities that cause you to want other people to think the way you want them to. Consider what you think of others and be aware of your own truths, knowing they may or may not reflect reality. Can you give yourself permission to be who you are without caring what other people think?

For a related message that will further clarify the situation, toss a coin three times:

3 Heads = 88   3 Tails = 38
1 Head and 2 Tails = 2   2 Heads and 1 Tail = 105

209
SUFFERING

ACCORDING TO BUDDHIST TEACHING, THE WORLD IS FULL OF SUF-
fering. Birth, old age, sickness and death are all sufferings. A
man full of hatred suffers, one separated from a loved one
suffers and someone vainly struggling to satisfy his or her
needs also suffers.

It is your resistance to what is that causes your suffering—
your desire for things to be other than what they are. In order
to rise above suffering, learn to recognize and accept what is,
and live your life by the precepts of the Eightfold Noble Path:
1. Right view; 2. Right thought; 3. Right speech; 4. Right
behavior; 5. Right livelihood; 6. Right effort; 7. Right mindfulness; and 8. Right concentration.

It is said that the Noble Path will lead you away from greed.
If you are free from greed, you will not quarrel with the world,
will not kill, steal, commit adultery, cheat, abuse, flatter, envy,
lose your temper, forget the transiency of life or be unjust.

Meditate upon how the Noble Path relates to your question
and the changes you need to make in your life.

For a related message that will further clarify the situation, toss a
coin three times:

3 Heads = 75   3 Tails = 241
1 Head and 2 Tails = 29   2 Heads and 1 Tail = 152

210
SERVING OTHERS

A SUFI TEACHING STORY TELLS OF A MAN WHO PRAYED CONTINU-
ally for the awareness to succeed in life. Then one night he
dreamed of going into the forest to attain understanding. The
next morning he went into the woods and wandered for several hours looking for some sign that would provide answers.
When he finally stopped to rest, he saw a fox with no legs
lying between two rocks in a cool place. Curious as to how a
legless fox could survive, he waited until sunset when he
observed a lion come and lay meat before the fox.

"Ah, I understand," the man thought. "The secret to success
in life is to trust that God will take care of all my needs. I
don't need to provide for myself. All I have to do is totally
surrender to my all-sustaining God."

Two weeks later, weakened and starving, the man had
another dream. In it he heard a voice say, "Fool. Be like the
lion, not like the fox."

Consider the value of serving others as it relates to your
question. St. Francis said, "It is in giving that we receive."

For a related message that will further clarify the situation, toss a
coin three times:

3 Heads = 180   3 Tails = 157
1 Head and 2 Tails = 242   2 Heads and 1 Tail = 190

211
BURDENS

ONCE THERE WAS A MAN ON A LONG JOURNEY WHO CAME TO A river. He said to himself: "This side of the river is very difficult and dangerous to walk on, and the other side seems easier and safer, but how shall I get across?" He built himself a raft out of branches and reeds and safely crossed the river. Then he thought to himself: "This raft has been very useful to me in crossing the river; I will not abandon it to rot on the bank, but will carry it along with me." Thus he voluntarily assumed an unnecessary burden. Can this man be called a wise man?

This parable teaches that even a good thing, when it becomes an unnecessary burden, should be thrown away; much more so if it is a bad thing.

Meditate upon the things you are carrying on your back that are not necessary. This includes even such things as useless and unnecessary discussions. Consider the changes in your life that would lighten your load and allow you to proceed at a brisker, freer pace.

For a related message that will further clarify the situation, toss a coin three times:

3 Heads = 22   3 Tails = 153
1 Head and 2 Tails = 204   2 Heads and 1 Tail = 9

212
DETACHED

BEING DETACHED DOES NOT MEAN YOU NEED BE LIFELESS OR DEAD to worldly passions. Your goal is to detach yourself from negativity so you can use all your time for creative expression, loving kindness, compassion, joy and meaningful learning.

When you detach from negativity, you let go of all emotions that program your subconscious mind in ways that will make life more difficult in the future. Thus you save yourself from wasting energy on unnecessary problems. To detach from negativity is the most logical thing to do for yourself to improve the quality of your life. Most problems begin as negative emotions that are magnified by your mind and projected into physical reality.

Meditate upon your need to rise above the effects of fear-based emotions, such as anger, greed, prejudice, hatred, cowardice, guilt, selfishness and jealousy. All of these emotions work against you and generate undesirable subconscious programming and undesirable karma that will keep you earthbound.

For a related message that will further clarify the situation, toss a coin three times:

3 Heads = 32   3 Tails = 209
1 Head and 2 Tails = 112   2 Heads and 1 Tail = 84

213
ARTIST & PAINTBRUSH

THINK OF YOUR HIGHER SELF AS AN ARTIST AND YOUR LOWER SELF as the picture you will paint. Your Higher Self is your karmically created character, and your lower self is your physical body—your traits, habits, and emotions. In each incarnation karma presents you, the artist, with an opportunity to paint your life picture. Do not confuse yourself with your picture. You are already a fully self-actualized, enlightened soul, who has only to project this awareness into your work.

You are forgetting that you are the artist and not the painting. You've allowed the painting to become your reality when you could be calling upon your buried talent to change the areas of the picture that are not working. You can erase portions of the picture and start again, painting a new image in bright, joyous colors.

Meditate upon picking up a paintbrush and painting your picture exactly the way that you want it to be. Visualize this very vividly and then project it into manifestation.

For a related message that will further clarify the situation, toss a coin three times:

3 Heads = 144

3 Tails = 59

1 Head and 2 Tails = 41

2 Heads and 1 Tail = 118

214
OBSTRUCTIONS

THE OBSTRUCTION IN YOUR PATH IS INHERENT IN YOUR CURRENT direction, and you must overcome it to accomplish your goals. Do not attempt to avoid it unless you are willing to give up all you hope to have. Do not attempt to encounter it directly for you do not yet have the strength to do so. Instead, stop and gather your awareness and strength to remove the obstruction.

Consider becoming like water that meets a rock in the stream. Water increases in volume and spills past the rock, eventually wearing it down. You may need to join forces with others, or align with established leaders to properly prepare to overcome this obstruction. You may need to be direct and honest with someone you don't want to hurt. Or you may need to yield to the obstruction, at least temporarily, to learn how to remove it.

Meditate upon what kind of obstruction you've established within yourself. If the source of the block is internal, you may have created it in the process of experiencing your inner conflicts. Or you may have purposely chosen this difficult path for the growth it offers. Regardless of the root of your obstructions, you will round out your character and increase self-esteem by handling the situation with unconditional love.

For a related message that will further clarify the situation, toss a coin three times:

3 Heads = 13   3 Tails = 208
1 Head and 2 Tails = 53   2 Heads and 1 Tail = 94

215
DIRECT & INDIRECT

YOUR RELATIONSHIPS ARE NOT FREE TO THE EXTENT THAT YOU demand things of other people. In making your day-to-day decisions, you always have a choice of actions, although you may be programmed to believe otherwise.

Consider your choices and the possible alternatives. Divide the choices into two categories—direct and indirect. Direct choices require only your involvement and action. Indirect choices demand the assistance and involvement of others.

Meditate upon how this relates to your question. Life is a quest for liberation, a quest for freedom. You will be better served when you act in ways that assist you to attain freedom of the self and from the self. Consider the demands you make upon other people in your life. How do you think they really feel about your needs? Consider the demands other people make upon you. How do you really feel about them? What changes can you make in your life to free up your relationships?

For a related message that will further clarify the situation, toss a coin three times:

3 Heads = 111
1 Head and 2 Tails = 38

3 Tails = 82
2 Heads and 1 Tail = 186

216
THE MIDDLE WAY

THINK ABOUT A LOG FLOATING IN A RIVER. IF THE LOG DOES NOT become grounded, or sink or decay, and is not taken out by a man, ultimately it will reach the sea. Life is like a log caught in the current of a great river. If a person does not become attached to a life of self-indulgence, or self-torture, if a person does not become proud of his virtues, become attached to his disharmonious acts or in his search for enlightenment does not become contemptuous of fear or delusion, such a person is following the Middle Way.

Avoid being caught and entangled in any extreme behavior. Don't get caught by pride of personality or praise for good deeds. Avoid being caught in the current of your desires or becoming attached to existence or to nonexistence. When you are too attached to things, a life of self-delusion begins.

Meditate upon how this relates to your question and upon any extremes in your life. Explore your attachments and decide if they are working for or against you. What delusions do they create?

For a related message that will further clarify the situation, toss a coin three times:

3 Heads = 36	3 Tails = 78
1 Head and 2 Tails = 156	2 Heads and 1 Tail = 44

217
ENLIGHTENMENT & DELUSION

ENLIGHTENMENT HAS NO DEFINITE FORM OR NATURE BY WHICH IT can manifest itself. Enlightenment exists solely because it's the polar opposite of delusion and ignorance; if they disappear, so will enlightenment. The reverse is also true: Delusion and ignorance only exist because of enlightenment. When enlightenment ceases, ignorance and delusion, too, will disappear.

Therefore, be on guard against thinking of enlightenment as a thing to be grasped, for it is like grasping water—the harder you grip, the faster it slips through your fingers. To grasp for this awareness means delusion remains with you. But when you are finally enlightened, you will come to know that everything is enlightenment. Before enlightenment, trees are just trees and men are just men. As you obtain enlightenment you perceive the transience of all forms and the illusion of reality. But once you have a full understanding, trees once again become trees and men once again become men. You accept everything is as it should be.

Meditate upon how your quest for enlightment and the delusions you are currently experiencing relate to your question.

For a related message that will further clarify the situation, toss a coin three times:

3 Heads = 219

3 Tails = 178

1 Head and 2 Tails = 183

2 Heads and 1 Tail = 158

218
ONLY GOD WILL BE LEFT

A JESUIT PRIEST WENT TO JAPAN TO STUDY IN A ZEN MONASTERY. He said that after sitting in meditation for long hours his legs would often begin to ache terribly. The master advised him on proper procedure and then asked what practice he was following in meditation. The Jesuit explained that he was sitting silently in the presence of God without words or thoughts or images or ideas. The master then asked if his God was everywhere. The Jesuit nodded his head, "yes." He asked if he was wrapped around in God, and the answer again was yes.

"Very good, very good," said the master. "Continue this way. Just keep on. And eventually you will find that God will disappear and only you will remain."

The Jesuit was offended by this for it sounded like a denial of his sacred beliefs. He contradicted the master and said, "God will not disappear. But I might disappear and only God will be left."

"Yes, yes," the master agreed, smiling. "It's the same thing. That is what I mean."

Meditate upon how your relationship with God and the concept of you being God, relates to your question.

For a related message that will further clarify the situation, toss a coin three times:

3 Heads = 167   3 Tails = 201
1 Head and 2 Tails = 177   2 Heads and 1 Tail = 248

219
UNCONSCIOUS SUFFERING

WHATEVER YOU REFUSE TO FACE CONSCIOUSLY YOU MUST SUFFER unconsciously. In fact all your current suffering is the result of situations you have refused to confront. You've refused to act, repressing your thoughts, feelings and emotions until they are like a rubber life raft held just below the surface of the water. You can stand on the emotional raft, forcing it down, but when you run out of energy to do that, or when you are not guarded, the repressed emotions surface and you experience the effects.

The only way to resolve the conflicts in your life is to deal with them as directly, honestly and efficiently as possible. This will result from: 1) acting self-responsibly; 2) learning to accept unalterable realities without dwelling on them; 3) developing the ability to consciously detach yourself from negativity; and 4) accepting that your life experience is based solely upon the way you choose to view what happens to you.

Meditate upon how this relates to your question and what you need to deal with directly and honestly.

For a related message that will further clarify the situation, toss a coin three times:

3 Heads = 177   3 Tails = 82
1 Head and 2 Tails = 240   2 heads and 1 Tail = 21

220
DUALITY

YOU FEAR MISFORTUNE AND DESIRE GOOD FORTUNE, BUT IF YOU carefully study the two, you find misfortune often turns out to be good fortune and good fortune to be misfortune. Learn to meet the changing circumstances of life with an equitable spirit. Do not be elated by success or depressed by failure.

Do not praise good and condemn bad, or cherish purity and despise impurity, or long for success and condemn failure. Recognize judging one thing against another is an expression of duality in your life.

Duality arises from false images in your mind. Be aware of all the words that express duality and eliminate them from your thinking and speech. When you can keep yourself free of these terms and the emotions they generate, you can begin to recognize what is and understand the truth in all things.

Meditate upon how duality is complicating your life. Exactly what are you judging? How is it working against you? What can you do to make it better?

For a related message that will further clarify the situation, toss a coin three times:

3 Heads = 149   3 Tails = 51
1 Head and 2 Tails = 170   2 Heads and 1 Tail = 223

221
SIMPLICITY

BECAUSE LIFE HAS BECOME SO COMPLICATED, MANY PEOPLE SEEK to simplify their existence in order to escape some of their pressures. It is comparatively easy to have few possessions and to be content with less. Many saints and gurus have chosen this path. But outward simplification isn't an answer unless you can change inwardly.

Your mind is a complicated network of interlocking and time-worn beliefs that are creating your current reality. When you can attain freedom from these beliefs you will experience simplicity, because what you are internally always manifests itself externally. As a simple person you would see much more directly than a complicated person, and you would become more sensitive to your surroundings, to the world, and to the problems that must be resolved.

Krishnamurti said, "Our problems—social, environmental, political, religious—are so complex that we can solve them only by being simple, not by becoming extraordinarily erudite and clever."

Meditate upon how simplifying your thinking relates to your question.

For a related message that will further clarify the situation, toss a coin three times:

3 heads = 57

3 Tails = 15

1 Head and 2 Tails = 1

2 Heads and 1 Tail = 228

222
SHARED LINEAGE

YOU ARE PART OF A SOUL GROUP THAT IS GATHERING TO SUPPORT shared goals. It is a reunion of those who were close in a past life and had a common philosophical basis of reality. During this gathering each member will slowly become known to the others. Although you cannot expect perfect harmony within the group, you will all sense the bond. This joint lineage will result in a strengthening of ancient ties and the power to accomplish tasks for the greater good of the group.

You must be open and receptive to those who share your energy and mentally commit to it wholeheartedly. Do all you can to encourage this unity without attempting to manipulate circumstances to serve yourself. As a result, you will notice an increased quality in your interaction with others. Be self-observant as you relate to the group; it will help you understand your common history and the purpose of reassembling at this time.

Meditate upon how others relate to your question and the potential effects of a soul group upon your goals.

For a related message that will further clarify the situation, toss a coin three times:

3 Heads = 110   3 Tails = 67

1 Head and 2 Tails = 88   2 Heads and 1 Tail = 171

223
WIN/WIN

MOST OF US WERE BROUGHT UP IN FAMILIES USING THE WIN/LOSE method of solving problems. You did what Mom and Dad said—or else. It was the same in schools when conflicts were resolved by an adult forcing obedience. We are not familiar with non-power methods of resolution because we've all experienced coercion and domination.

Yet a problem is not resolved on a karmic level unless both people win or both sides win. A win/win approach to problems produces a solution that satisfies our mutual needs. There is nothing new about it: We often use it with friends or non-power-oriented relationships. But we don't use win/win posturing where there are obvious power differentials such as boss/subordinate, teacher/student, parent/child and sometimes even in our primary relationship.

Consider how to resolve all conflicts with win/win solutions. Figure out how both parties can keep their self-esteem and uphold each others' rights. Allow each party to be part of the decision making process. Have both sides share in the responsibility and commitment. Win/win solutions require trade-offs and they take more time initially, but the results will be worthwhile in the end.

For a related message that will further clarify the situation, toss a coin three times:

3 Heads = 248   3 Tails = 217
1 Head and 2 Tails = 59   2 Heads and 1 Tail = 2

224
ISOLATION

YOUR LIFE IS AN EXPERIENCE COMPRISED OF RELATIONSHIPS IN action because no one really lives in isolation. Only through your relationships can you come to know yourself and experience who you are. Yet most relationships involve processes of isolation. Although you claim to care about others, in fact you are only willing to relate to another person as long as the relationship serves you. When there are problems that cause you discomfort, you will be ready to discard this relationship. The relationship exists only as long as you experience personal gratification. It follows that if relationships follow a process of isolation, how can society be anything but isolated? How can the world be anything else?

The key to changing your relationships, society and the world begin with self-understanding. Get to know yourself, explore your motives, intents and desires. You'll find fear is always the problem: fear that the relationship won't allow you to get what you want; fear that you won't receive approval; fear that someone will ask too much of you; fear that the other person won't be what you want them to be.

With this awareness in mind, consider accepting others without expectations. Accept self-responsibility and attempt to view every relationship from a perspective of unconditional love.

For a related message that will further clarify the situation, toss a coin three times:

3 Heads = 189   3 Tails = 98
1 Head and 2 Tails = 249   2 Heads and 1 Tail = 137

225
GOSSIP

WHEN YOU NEED TO KNOW WHAT OTHERS ARE SAYING OR DOING, your inquisitive mind is being misguided and is acting superficially. You think gossip will somehow reveal another person to you, but how can you know this person if you don't know yourself? What is the value of gossip other than escaping from yourself? Does it mask your desire to interfere in the lives of others? Or is it a behind-the-back judgment you don't have the nerve to deliver directly?

Whenever you discuss another person negatively you generate karma. Your thoughts and words are subconscious programming that will always come back to you in the form of negative experiences. To stop gossiping, you simply have to become aware of the fact you are doing it and decide to stop judging others. When a friend starts gossiping, say, "I can't judge her. She may not be doing the best she can, but she's doing the best she knows how." You might also say, "I've decided to stop dwelling upon anything negative, so let's talk about something else." Or, "I don't agree with the choice he is making but I support his right to make it." Or say, "Let's just accept what she is. She may not be living up to what we see as her potential, but she isn't on this earth to please us."

How does the gossip surrounding you relate to your question?

For a related message that will further clarify the situation, toss a coin three times:

3 Heads = 88   3 Tails = 35
1 Head and 2 Tails = 60   2 Heads and 1 Tail = 204

226
EXAMINE YOUR MOTIVES

WHAT IS THE MOTIVE BEHIND THE DESIRE THAT HAS CAUSED YOU to ask your question? You often fool yourself as to why you want something. You think you have an obvious reason, while the real motivation hides in the shadows of your mind, hoping to avoid detection.

All desire is self-serving. Even if you only want to help the disadvantaged, your motive is self-serving because your actions allow you to feel better about yourself. But when your self-serving desires harm or manipulate others, you have crossed a line that will incur karmic debts. Metaphysical teachers often use an example of countries at war to show the subtlety of this. If you desire your country to win, you pray for victory. But is this not a mental projection of "black power," because you are praying for the other side to lose?

You desire to have a relationship that fulfills you, but does it serve the other person? You want success, but at what cost to others? You want something because your mate or parents or children expect you to want it, but at what cost to you? Meditate on all the hidden motives behind your question.

For a related message that will further clarify the situation, toss a coin three times:

3 Heads = 97   3 Tails = 105
1 Head and 2 Tails = 153   2 Heads and 1 Tail = 123

243

227
PROJECTING CHARACTER

IF YOU ARE TRULY RELIGIOUS, YOU DON'T NEED TO PRACTICE YOUR religion—you live it. Religion is like breathing; you are not aware of breathing unless you think about it, or something goes wrong. To a religious person, religion is not a discipline, but rather an awareness. It isn't something that is imposed from the outside; it flows from within, leaving no space between you and your religion.

To project religious convictions and make a show of the outward practice of religion is merely a device of the nonreligious to avoid religion. Most religion, however, is based on fear, such as fear of a sadistic God who throws people into hell. Can a religion based on fear be true?

The truly religious man accepts karma and seeks to rise above fear. He no longer judges or blames others. He is a compassionate man. He doesn't talk about God because he *lives* God, enjoys God, celebrates God. He exists in the present and lives totally.

What kind of religious character are you projecting? How does this relate to your question and the way you are living your life?

For a related message that will further clarify the situation, toss a coin three times:

3 heads = 105   3 Tails = 227
1 Head and 2 Tails = 112   2 Heads and 1 Tail = 136

244

228
YOUR NATURE

A TEACHING PARABLE TELLS OF A TURTLE WARMING ITSELF ON THE beach when it sighted a large, ugly-looking scorpion crawling toward her with its deadly tail curled to strike. Without hesitating, the turtle crawled to the safety of the water.

"Please, wait," cried the scorpion. "I won't hurt you. I need to get to that island over there. Please give me a ride."

The turtle, now at the water's edge, trembled in horror. "No way. You're a scorpion. You'll sting me and I'll die."

"No, I won't," the scorpion said sadly. "I only sting to catch food. I certainly wouldn't hurt someone who helped me. Everybody fears me and nobody trusts me," he sobbed.

Moved by the pleading, the turtle became sympathetic and finally said, "All right, if you promise not to sting me."

Gratefully promising, the scorpion climbed on the turtle's back and rode safely across the sea to the island. As the scorpion climbed down onto the island sand it viciously stung the turtle. "But you promised not to hurt me." The turtle gasped as the deadly poison coursed through its body.

As the scorpion walked away, it turned to laugh and said, "But it's my nature to sting."

Meditate upon the nature of those relating to your question.

For a related message that will further clarify the situation, toss a coin three times:

3 Heads = 155   3 Tails = 90
1 Head and 2 Tails = 250   2 Heads and 1 Tail = 48

229
REPLACING ILLUSIONS

YOU LIVE IN AN ILLUSION CREATED BY THE WAY YOU VIEW WHAT happens to you. The illusion is the result of all your previous experiences being projected into the current situation.

There is a Zen story about a man who was sitting in the middle of the road drawing his arms forward and back as if rowing a boat.

Since he was blocking the road, a traveler asked him, "What are you doing? Are you crazy?"

"I'm rowing a boat," replied the man. "I have room for you if you want to join me."

"But there is no boat," said the traveler.

"No boat? Oh my God, we'd better start swimming," replied the panicked man.

When you finally realize the illusion, do not immediately create another one. It is time to explore what is—what is reality and what is illusion, what can be changed and what cannot be changed. It is time to recognize the difference.

For a related message that will further clarify the situation, toss a coin three times:

3 Heads = 212

1 Head and 2 Tails = 177

3 Tails = 96

2 Heads and 1 Tail = 169

230
MISUNDERSTANDING

IN A DIM LIGHT YOU MIGHT SEE A LENGTH OF ROPE LYING ON THE ground and believe it to be a snake. The snake is not real, but your mind projects the fear as real. Naturally, you respond to the fear. Maybe you tremble. Maybe you run and fall. You could even have a heart attack and die. But all the while there was never any snake at all. You created and projected it into reality.

It follows that your familiar world is not real. It is simply your projection of the world, which is why the eastern mystic calls it *maya*—an illusion. Yes, the world exists, but your mind distorts it and creates great misunderstandings. Your conscious beliefs about philosophy, relationships and society confuse it further, and your deeper beliefs about who and what you are blur reality even more.

If your mind is wrong, maybe no-mind is right. No-mind would be a matter of ceasing to compare one thing or person to another. No division. No prejudice. No judgment. No blame. It would mean you accept the unalterable realities. There would be no past and no future—only now.

Meditate upon comparisons and illusions as they relate to your question and how they could affect the manifestation of your desires.

For a related message that will further clarify the situation, toss a coin three times:

3 Heads = 164   3 Tails = 102
1 Head and 2 Tails = 101   2 Heads and 1 Tail = 17

231
ACCURATE COMMUNICATION

YOUR PERCEPTION OF THE CURRENT SITUATION IS NOT NECESSARILY shared by others. We each hear words and view situations through our filters of past experience.

Osho tells the story of a man with a wooden eye who attended a community dance. He was so self-conscious about his wooden eye that he didn't mix with the others. He stood alone, off to the side, feeling sad and lonely, watching other people enjoying themselves. Then he noticed a girl with a large wart on her nose who was also alone.

"Maybe she would dance with me," thought the man.

He gathered his courage and approached the woman. "Would you . . . would you like to dance with me?" he stammered.

Her face brightened. "Would I? Would I?" she cried.

Offended, the man drew back. "Wart nose. Wart nose," he countered.

How does this story relate to your question. Meditate upon the way others may be interpreting your communications.

For a related message that will further clarify the situation, toss a coin three times:

3 Heads = 167   3 Tails = 234
1 Head and 2 Tails = 52 2 Heads and 1 Tail = 125

232
ADVANCEMENT

THE UNIVERSAL FORCES ARE RELEASING GREAT ENERGY INTO YOUR current situation. As a result, all things may be possible at this time. Make the best of the positive energy while it lasts. Seek to accomplish your goals as long as they are worthwhile and will serve more than yourself.

It may be necessary for you to make personal sacrifices to advance the goals, but in so doing you will benefit yourself and society as well. Others will be impressed by your actions and support you in turn.

The universal forces surrounding you will also support any and all self-improvement endeavors. If you desire to break old habits or develop new abilities, do so now. Also consider discarding your negative thinking and self-indulgent attitudes. Establish a solid new foundation based upon self-realization and the higher principles. Become aware of the positive results generated by compassionate people and seek to emulate their ways. Become a channel for the light and your entire life will be transformed.

For a related message that will further clarify the situation, toss a coin three times:

3 heads = 159	3 Tails = 33
1 Head and 2 Tails = 8	2 Heads and 1 Tail = 226

233
ULTIMATE WISDOM

ALL OF THE AWARENESS IN THIS BOOK CAN BE SIMPLIFIED DOWN TO four words: *Cast away your delusions.* This is the ultimate wisdom—the way to eliminate suffering, the formula for enlightenment.

All your fear-based emotions are delusions: prejudice, selfishness, hate, repression, envy, greed, possessiveness, inhibitions and guilt are all responses to past programming. These undesirable, unnecessary fears keep you earthbound on the wheel of reincarnation. But beneath your programming, you are already a fully enlightened soul, so the goal is to cast away your delusions so you can more fully realize what you already are.

This wisdom includes, "loving yourself and others," and "loving unconditionally," because underneath your delusions you are pure love—beyond judgment, blame and expectations. Without delusions you would accept what is.

Meditate upon your delusions that need to be cast away, especially as they relate to your question. Relate your fear-based emotions to the concept and explore how this knowledge could change your life.

For a related message that will further clarify the situation, toss a coin three times:

3 Heads = 116   3 Tails = 19
1 Head and 2 Tails = 4   2 Heads and 1 Tail = 223

234
THE TEN PRECEPTS

ZEN TEACHES THAT THERE ARE TEN PRECEPTS OF MORAL CONDUCT
to accelerate the process of liberation: 1. Not to kill—and help
yourself to really live by developing awareness. 2. Not to
steal—and give to others. 3. Not to misuse sexuality—when
having sex with another you must consider your happiness,
that of your companion and of the third person who will be
most affected by the act. If these three people can be satisfied,
then sex falls within the natural law of human beings. 4. Not
to lie—and also avoid the lie of pride. 5. Not to misuse intoxicants—do not harm the health of your body or mind by using
intoxicants to excess. 6. Not to slander—shun gossip and slander.
Be truthful and loving with your words. 7. Not to insult—never
purposefully hurt another with words. 8. Not to covet—never
want more than you need, nor be greedy and ungenerous
toward others in need. 9. Not to anger—anger is always a
protection against pain, resulting from you not getting what
you want. 10. Not to slander the All That Is—become aware
that we are the All.

Meditate upon how the Ten Precepts of moral conduct relate
to your question, and how you can integrate this awareness
into the fulfillment of your aspirations.

For a related message that will further clarify the situation, toss a
coin three times:

3 Heads = 22   3 Tails = 128
1 Head and 2 Tails = 75   2 Heads and 1 Tail = 49

235
LIVING CONSCIOUSLY

BY LIVING UNCONSCIOUSLY, YOU GO THROUGH THE MOTIONS OF life. You go from one job to the next—you change mates, hobbies, religions in the hope that this time something is going to happen. You live for expectations, thinking, "This time I'll pull it off. This time if I make these changes it will happen. This time it will be great. This time I'll be happy."

But unless you can start living consciously, without expectations, nothing is going to happen. Until you can consciously know yourself and cast away your delusions, nothing will change. It is time to explore why you do what you do. Explore your patterns and discover why you repeat them, or you will be frustrated again and again and you will miss the meaning of life.

Rather than changing the people and things in your life, consider changing your consciousness in ways that will allow you to stop clinging to expectations and illusions. Were your past expectations based upon what is? What about your current expectations?

For a related message that will further clarify the situation, toss a coin three times:

3 Heads = 7

3 Tails = 182

1 Head and 2 Tails = 128

2 Heads and 1 Tail = 111

236
A WISHING TREE

THERE IS A PARABLE ABOUT A POOR MAN WALKING THROUGH THE woods reflecting upon his many troubles. He stopped to rest against a tree, a magical tree that would instantly grant the wishes of anyone who came in contact with it. He realized he was thirsty and wished for a drink. Instantly a cup of cool water was in his hand. Shocked, he looked at the water, decided it was safe and drank it. He then realized he was hungry and wished he had something to eat. A meal appeared before him.

"My wishes are being granted," he thought in disbelief. "Well, then I wish for a beautiful home of my own," he said out loud. The home appeared in the meadow before him. A huge smile crossed his face as he wished for servants to take care of the house. When they appeared he realized he had somehow been blessed with an incredible power and he wished for a beautiful, loving, intelligent woman to share his good fortune.

"Wait a minute, this is ridiculous," said the man to the woman. "I'm not this lucky. This can't happen to me." As he spoke everything disappeared. He shook his head and said, "I knew it," then walked away thinking about his many troubles.

Thoughts are things and they create your reality. Meditate upon how this story relates to your question.

For a related message that will further clarify the situation, toss a coin three times:

3 Heads = 37   3 Tails = 13
1 Head and 2 Tails = 23   2 Heads and 1 Tail = 16

237
THE SIX PERFECTIONS

THE SIX BUDDHIST PERFECTIONS OFFER GUIDELINES TO ALL SEEKERS of self-advancement. 1. Giving. There are three kinds of giving—the giving of materials, of awareness and of "unafraidness,"—risking yourself to save others from disaster or misfortune. 2. Keep the precepts. Do not kill. Do not steal. Do not misuse sexuality. Do not lie. Do not misuse intoxicants. Do not slander. Do not insult. Do not covet. Do not anger. Do not slander the All That Is. 3. Perseverance. The world includes suffering, but we must persevere and rise above the suffering, physically as well as mentally. 4. Assiduity. Exert the diligence to avoid doing anything disharmonious and to do everything harmoniously. Nothing is completed without diligence. Because we are part of society, we work for money, name and position. But we must realize that our real work has nothing to do with these things, and should be directed to creating harmony on this earth. 5. Meditation. By going within on a regular basis, you awaken the True Self. 6. Transcendantal wisdom. This is wisdom that transcends the knowledge of things and of the mind. It transcends all dualities to become illumination.

Meditate upon how the Six Perfections relate to your question and how you can merge the awareness into your goals.

For a related message that will further clarify the situation, toss a coin three times:

3 Heads = 221   3 Tails = 96
1 Head and 2 Tails = 98   2 Heads and 1 Tail = 8

238
SELF-TESTING KARMA

YOUR CURRENT SITUATION IS KARMIC. ALL KARMA EITHER rewards or balances past deeds and then tests you to see if you have learned your lessons. For example, you might have been blessed with a good marriage. Your test comes when the marriage hits a bumpy road. How do the two of you handle it? If you both respond with compassion, chances are you'll remain together happily and won't experience the long-term pain of parting that could have resulted if you hadn't learned your lessons.

From another perspective, let's assume you lack compassion, leave your mate and take up with someone new. You have probably failed your own test and will someday find yourself abandoned in a similar situation.

But what if your mate leaves you and you handle the parting without anger, letting go in a supportive way? You've probably passed the test, and at the same time, paid off old karma by being left.

The outcome of self-testing karma isn't predestined because you have free will. Your question may not have anything to do with relationships, but self-testing karma is a factor. Meditate upon how testing yourself may relate to your inquiry.

For a related message that will further clarify the situation, toss a coin three times:

3 Heads = 248
1 Head and 2 Tails = 46

3 Tails = 137
2 Heads and 1 Tail = 157

239
SOUL GOALS

BEFORE YOU WERE BORN YOU ESTABLISHED SOUL GOAL PRIORITIES, ranking their importance. There are seven general goal areas: 1. Attain Knowledge. This wisdom could include the desire for direct knowledge of humility, devotion, sacrifice, selflessness or perseverance. 2. Open Spiritually. Integrate spiritual awareness into your chosen life work. 3. Achieve Inner Harmony. Be involved with the world and the accomplishment of your life work while at the same time attaining peace of mind. 4. Attain Fame or Power. Both are karmic rewards as well as tests, and offer unique opportunities to communicate awareness and exert leadership. 5. Learn Acceptance. Overcome your resistance to what is which causes your suffering. 6. Provide Support. Nurture another person, an ideal or a philosophical or religious belief. 7. Develop Talent. Talents are developed over many lifetimes. The goal could be in the beginning, intermediary or advanced stage of creative pursuit.

One of these seven goals is most important to you. Combined with an awareness of your dharma, which is your duty to yourself and society, knowledge of your soul goal will help you understand your earthly purpose. Meditate upon your primary soul goal and how it relates to your question.

For a related message that will further clarify the situation, toss a coin three times:

3 Heads = 199   3 Tails = 7
1 Head and 2 Tails = 59   2 Heads and 1 Tail = 137

240
TEMPTATION

ALTHOUGH IT MAY NOT SEEM SO ON THE SURFACE, A DISHARMONI-
ous temptation is involved in the situation you question. If you
are not careful in how you respond, you could create chaos in
your life and alter your destiny. Although there is little you
can do to remove the temptation, you have the free will to
prevent it from gaining power over you. You know in your
heart what you must do to avoid acting with intent and generating undesirable karma.

In all social situations you will need to be diplomatic and
careful. Let others know how you feel. Confront any issue that
could be used against you. In your career, be sure that your
efforts are not counterproductive. Considering the temptation,
any unorthodox decisions could create more problems than
benefits.

You may come face-to-face with a new indulgence, which
might appear to be harmless, but has the potential to develop
into a disharmonious character trait or internal disturbance. If
this is the case, you will need to exert a great deal of self-
discipline to avoid being pulled under. Hold on to your higher
principles. Unconditionally love yourself and draw upon your
inner strength.

For a related message that will further clarify the situation, toss a
coin three times:

3 heads = 213   3 Tails = 26
1 Head and 2 Tails = 4   2 Heads and 1 Tail = 70

241
RESPONSIBILITY

① RESPONSIBILITY IS THE BASIS OF TRANSFORMATION. THE ACCEPT-
ance of karma is the acceptance of responsibility for past
thoughts, words and deeds that have created your current reality. If your life doesn't work, if it is chaotic, oppressive or filled
with anguish, take responsibility for it. But know that if you
have created your life the way it is, you have the ability to
create it exactly as you desire it to be.

② Responsibility also means the capacity to respond as a fully
conscious, awakened individual. It means to be fully alert,
aware and conscious—to be mindful. Infuse this awareness
into everything that you do, even the small things, such as
walking, driving, eating and bathing. Do them all with full
awareness. These small acts are like seeds that will take root
and begin to sprout within you, until they flower into your
full potential. When you are totally aware, it transforms the
way you experience your life.

Meditate upon how both kinds of responsibility relate to
your question.

For a related message that will further clarify the situation, toss a
coin three times:

3 Heads = 182   3 Tails = 67
1 Head and 2 Tails = 48   2 Heads and 1 Tail = 193

242
THROUGH MIND/
WITHOUT MIND

UPON ATTAINING TRANSFORMATION, SELF-ACTUALIZATION, *SATORI*, enlightenment, illumination or whatever term you care to use to describe enhanced awareness, you may find you are a stranger to those around you. Your differences may be so great that others will be unable to understand you. You will be considered an outsider, weird or dangerous by those who live with an attached mind—through the mind. You live with a detached mind—without the mind. You will understand them because once you lived as they live.

You've known both lives. But how do you communicate an awareness that you know to be inexpressible? How can you expect others to understand someone who stops judging them, stops blaming them and stops having expectations of them? When you accept others as they are without manipulation, or giving advice, or expectations of change, they may not be able to relate to you. This is such an alien concept it may make them nervous.

Your acceptance of self-responsibility will be even more difficult to fathom, and they will not understand your refusal to be subjected to any form of negativity. Your acceptance of what is, and your positive viewpoint will complete the image of a stranger among them. Meditate upon how this understanding relates to your question.

For a related message that will further clarify the situation, toss a coin three times:

3 Heads = 9   3 Tails = 235
1 Head and 2 Tails = 2   2 Heads and 1 Tail = 78

243
ACCEPT YOUR NATURE

THERE IS NO ONE WAY THAT IS RIGHT FOR EVERYONE—NO PERFECT diet, no set hours of sleep, no ideal level of stress. Osho says that some people are tortoises, others are hares. If the hare isn't allowed to do things with speed, he will experience stress. His natural pace is for speed, and he isn't interested in relaxation. His joy is generated by racing. If the turtle tries to become a hare, he will have trouble, too.

Accept your nature. If being a warrior is natural for you, then it is your dharma. You will find your joy in being a warrior, but that doesn't mean you can't be an enlightened warrior. Do not accept your nature timidly—embrace it wholeheartedly. Be who you are completely.

When you really understand who you are, make it all right with yourself to be this way. It will help you clarify your relationship with others and explain why communication is often more difficult than it needs to be.

Meditate upon how being who you really are relates to your question. Consider your need for self-acceptance and make any changes in attitude that might better serve you.

For a related message that will further clarify the situation, toss a coin three times:

3 Heads = 229

3 Tails = 161

1 Head and 2 Tails = 3

2 Heads and 1 Tail = 84

244
ENDURING EFFORT

YOUR CURRENT SITUATION CAN BE AFFECTED ONLY BY FOCUSING upon and gradually working toward your goal. Do not attempt to force or pressure your way to a situation. It simply won't work and could create a complication or total reversal of circumstances.

You need to clarify your intent and apply gradual effort over a long period of time. Emulate the water that wears away a rock in the stream. If you must influence others, perceive the spirit of that group and align yourself with their concerns, hopes and dreams. Although it will take time, you will make a profound impression. The same is now true of your personal relationships. Be patient and think in terms of lengthy commitments.

Make your decisions and then stick to them. Great accomplishments will result from an enduring effort focused upon a clearly defined goal. Remember that thoughts are things and they create, so always remain optimistic about the successful fulfillment of your desires.

For a related message that will further clarify the situation, toss a coin three times:

3 Heads = 97   3 Tails = 119
1 Head and 2 Tails = 75   2 Heads and 1 Tail = 250

245
MORE SILENCE

WITH THE RARE EXCEPTION OF A STATEMENT OF FACT, OR A QUES-
tion requiring a factual answer, everything you say is to attain
sympathy or to make yourself more important. You don't like
to hear that, but a little self-monitoring will demonstrate it's
true. Recognizing this will help you become aware of your
phoniness, by forcing you to observe your projected insecurity.

If you aren't talking to someone else, you are in a continual
dialogue with yourself. While you are monitoring your words
to see if you want sympathy or importance, observe that ninety
percent of your talking is useless. If you give up the ninety
percent and use only the remaining ten percent, you will
become a more effective communicator. An unnecessary burden will be lifted.

Osho says silence is "looking into existence directly, immediately. You are in contact with existence without anything in
between you and existence."

Why not stop thinking and talking about unnecessary
things? This reduction in inner and outer chatter will allow you
to put aside some of your mental furnishings—your desires,
memories, fantasies and dreams. Look directly into your
existence.

For a related message that will further clarify the situation, toss a
coin three times:

3 Heads = 216   3 Tails = 24
1 Head and 2 Tails = 122   2 Heads and 1 Tail = 225

246
CONTRADICTION

INTELLECTUALS DEMAND CONSISTENCY, BUT ANYONE WHO COULD remain consistent over an entire life would be as rigid and interesting as a fence post. To evolve and grow you will have to contradict yourself many times. One of your basic rights is the right to change your mind. What works for you today may not work tomorrow. What you liked last year may not appeal to you today, or maybe you just got tired of living that life-style and changed.

Changing your mind is healthy and normal, but other people may challenge your right to do so. They will want explanations and an admission that your first choice was a mistake. "How could you change your mind after you committed yourself? You're irresponsible and will probably make a faulty decision next time." Don't accept such rigid thinking and blatant manipulation.

If you are contradictory and change your mind, it may be because you are vast enough to contain paradoxes. Meditate upon your question as it relates to contradiction.

For a related message that will further clarify the situation, toss a coin three times:

3 Heads = 218   3 Tails = 175
1 Head and 2 Tails = 181   2 Heads and 1 Tail = 35

247
UNACCEPTABLES

IF YOU ARE UPSET BY UNACCEPTABLE THINGS, ALL YOU HAVE TO do to resolve the situation is accept what seems unacceptable. These things are not unacceptable to everyone else—not to society, not to God—just to you. Examine your unacceptables until you clearly understand they exist as a personal issue only because you give them power. Understand that you empower them by choosing to view them in a certain way.

Of course, you don't have to give up the unacceptables in your life, but you will suffer as a result of each one you cling to. Each unacceptable will continue to upset you as long as you hold it or try to push it away.

To free yourself, simply accept all your unacceptables. To try to change the situation is usually a waste of time. It doesn't work or it makes matters worse. Accept what is, and make it okay. Just say "yes" to the way things are.

Meditate upon what you find unacceptable in your life and how this relates to your question.

For a related message that will further clarify the situation, toss a coin three times:

3 Heads = 145   3 Tails = 50
1 Head and 2 Tails = 113   2 Heads and 1 Tail = 132

248
INSPIRATION

NOW YOU CAN INSPIRE OTHERS TO COOPERATE AND TO BECOME more than they think they can be. The universal forces will favor any inspirational efforts you care to make during this period of enhanced power. You must simply remain aware of the truth and show compassion in all your interactions. Your efforts will generate loyalty, commitment and long-term support.

This power extends into your personal relationships as well, and you will be able to communicate more deeply than you might believe possible. Remain focused upon your goals as you inspire those close to you, openly discussing where you desire to guide them. Make sure your motives, intents and desires are positive.

Your success as it relates to your question will depend upon your ability to create and maintain an environment of trust, compassion and gentleness that will carry you safely across the sea of ever-changing external conditions. Your integrity and commitment to higher principles will keep you from being tempted by distractions unworthy of your concern.

For a related message that will further clarify the situation, toss a coin three times:

3 Heads = 27   3 Tails = 69
1 Head and 2 Tails = 218   2 Heads and 1 Tail = 186

249
FACTS DO NOT
CHANGE ATTITUDES

A SUFI TEACHING STORY TELLS OF A TRAVELER WHO WAS CROSSING a strange world known as the Land of Fools. While walking down a rural road he observed farmers fleeing in terror. "There's a monster in that field," said a man as he ran past.

The traveler looked out into the field and saw a watermelon. So he called the farmers together and offered to kill the monster for them. He then walked into the field, took out a knife and cut the melon in half and started to eat it. The farmers were horrified and feared the traveler more than they had the watermelon. They drove him out of their world with pitchforks, screaming, "He'll kill us next if we don't get rid of him."

The following season another traveler found himself journeying through the same world, and the same thing happened to him. But instead of offering to kill the monster, he agreed with them that it was dangerous, and by tiptoeing away from it with them he gained their confidence. He spent time in their homes until he could teach them, a little at a time, the facts that would allow them to rise above their fear of watermelons and cultivate the melons themselves.

The truth alone does not make people free. Meditate upon this and how the story relates to your question.

For a related message that will further clarify the situation, toss a coin three times:

3 Heads = 8

1 Head and 2 Tails = 243

3 Tails = 102

2 Heads and 1 Tail = 127

250
WHY BELIEVE

WHY BELIEVE IN GOD WHEN YOU CAN EXPERIENCE GOD? BELIEF IS a poor substitute for experience. If you want to know, don't simply believe. You can only believe things you don't actually know. You may believe your mate is faithful. You believe it with all your heart, but you don't know because you are not with your mate every moment of every day. You believe in reincarnation, but you can't be certain you will be reborn. You believe your country is right, but that may not be what is. Intellectually, you are convinced because you cannot accept any argument that will destroy your belief.

But beliefs are like medicines, and healthy people don't need medicine. The believer is the superficial part of you that believes you have something to fear. It generates your prejudicial beliefs, your possessive beliefs, your greedy beliefs, your hateful beliefs and all other beliefs based in fear.

Do not disbelieve, either, for it is simply another form of belief. Meditate upon belief as a bondage to transcend and consider how this relates to your question.

For a related message that will further clarify the situation, toss a coin three times:

3 Heads = 138   3 Tails = 31
1 Head and 2 Tails = 187   2 Heads and 1 Tail = 154

DICK SUTPHEN publishes *Master of Life* magazine, a free quarterly that keeps readers abreast of his latest research and findings. To receive a copy, please write to:

Dick Sutphen
Box 38
Malibu, CA 90265